2-4 5 7

A Simple Guide
to Prayer

A Simple Guide
to Prayer

JOHN UNDERWOOD STEPHENS

ABINGDON PRESS
New York   Nashville

A SIMPLE GUIDE TO PRAYER

Copyright © MCMLVII by Abingdon Press

Library of Congress Catalog Card Number: 57-5281

Scripture quotations so designated are from the Revised
Standard Version of the Bible and are copyright 1946
and 1952 by the Division of Christian Education of the
National Council of the Churches of Christ in the U.S.A.

SET UP, PRINTED, AND BOUND BY THE
PARTHENON PRESS, AT NASHVILLE,
TENNESSEE, UNITED STATES OF AMERICA

TO

Carol Underwood Stephens

my first grandchild
and to her parents Wade and Jean
with daily thanksgiving and intercession
in their threefold behalf

PREFACE

THIS IS INTENDED TO BE A SIMPLE, PRACTICAL BOOK THAT all men who can read at all can read with profit: a book that moves rapidly along in such wise as to interest equally the layman and the theologian.

A Simple Guide to Prayer is designed to meet a number of specific needs: (1) the need of those who are strangers to prayer, who desire to enter into the rewarding experience of praying; (2) the need of those whose prayers have been a treading of the mill of routine, who long to find through prayer the wealth of heaven brought into the heart; (3) the need of those whose prayers, although unquestionably alive and active, have yet to grow into the stature of adulthood: strong, resourceful, wise, and able; (4) the need of those, long acquainted with prayer's ways, who look for some refreshment and encouragement of fellowship, howbeit through the printed page, with a kindred mind; (5) the need of every man, of every stage of learning, for books whose very reading shall, in however modest measure, constitute a drawing-near to God.

This book is written from within, that if possible it may fathom the "within" of its reader. It speaks in pictures and parables, that truth may be clad with flesh and blood. It

7

abounds in biblical allusion and quotation, that windows may be opened upon the Scriptures. And, since the book results from personal experience and observation, its essential nature is that of confession and description rather than of argument or theory.

A short list of helpful books on the subjects of prayer and the Bible, with brief notes about each book, appears under the heading "Some Aids to Prayer." These books can be purchased at almost any bookstore, at least in the United States; for most bookdealers will gladly order for a customer any book that is currently in print, and some dealers will advertise for a book that is out of print. Out-of-print books, moreover, can occasionally be found in stores that specialize in secondhand books.

Thanks are due to friends and family for many kinds of help. Dr. George A. Buttrick, in addition to other friendly kindnesses, has favored me with penetrating criticism of the temporarily completed manuscript. This has led to much rewriting and improvement. But if anything in this book be blameworthy, it is mine and not his.

My lifelong friend Miss Alice Lightbourn, of Pittsfield, Massachusetts, has been persuaded to make helpful suggestions from the layman's point of view. Several of these have influenced the text.

Mr. Charles E. Campbell, of Portland, Maine, has kindly furnished information as to the present availability of books mentioned under "Some Aids to Prayer."

My son Wade C. Stephens, and his wife, Jean S. Stephens, have contributed a thought here and a thought there, for which this book is better than it would otherwise have been.

My son Horace D. Stephens has helped likewise. He has also spent many hours trying to find the unfindable source of that brief quotation on page eighteen.

My wife, Louise K. Stephens, has made contribution measurable only by the limits of this book. Her daily care, her patience, her faith and wisdom and encouragement, have been large ingredients in this endeavor. The book, it seems to me, is hers almost as much as it is mine.

JOHN UNDERWOOD STEPHENS

CONTENTS

I

Who Can Pray?

✳✳✳✳✳✳✳✳✳✳✳✳✳✳✳✳✳✳✳✳✳✳✳✳✳✳✳✳✳✳✳✳✳✳✳✳

Probably anyone who can breathe can pray.

Prayer is the breathing of a living soul.

SOMETIMES, TO BE SURE, WE PRAY SO SLIGHTLY THAT WE ARE
unaware that we pray at all. Then we are like that small
boy who thought that breathing occurred only when he
heard it. "See!" he would exclaim, "I haven't breathed
for half an hour!"

Yet if he had really stopped breathing, he would have
stopping saying that he had stopped. Moreover, he could
breathe deeply when he wished only because he breathed
after a fashion whether he would or not. It is likewise with
prayer. Conscious prayer can never be wholly strange to
him who has already prayed unconsciously.

How indeed should we know God when we seek and
find him, if we had not unknowingly known him all
along? Here is the outreach of God's lowliness and the
touch of his compassion: that even while we deny him he
gives us food and drink; when we flee his face he fills the
night which we had hoped would cover us; and though our
lips be sealed until no syllable of prayer escapes them,

the whisper of God persists within our heart. Accordingly Isaiah says, in phrase of surpassing loveliness, as from the very mouth of God, "I am found of them that sought me not" (65:1). This is the beginning of prayer.

The conscious turning of the life toward God is, then, not prayer's beginning but prayer's growth. Here is a parable: a grain of wheat, taken from an Egyptian tomb that had been closed for three thousand years, has grown in this latter day. Surrounded at last by warmth and moisture, the little germ of life, apparently extinct for three milleniums, has revived and put forth a shoot. Upon first thought, the wonder of such persistence of life may overshadow another fact no less significant. This further fact is that growth, when finally it does occur, is not an original action. It is a motion of response.

The lengthening stalk of wheat, reaching toward the light, is not attempting to create the sun or even to attract it, but is rising to weclome the sunlight that has already quickened it. Even so, when a man prays, he originates nothing. He neither creates God nor of his own initiative attracts the attention of God. Rather he turns to welcome God, because God has made him alive.

This healthful and hopeful responsiveness of prayer is seen in the almost incredulous joy of the psalmist who prayed, "When thou saidest, Seek ye my face; my heart said unto thee, Thy face, Lord, will I seek" (27:8). Thus the beginning of prayer is always the besieging of the soul by God. The besieging of God by the soul is prayer's completion.

Here is comfort for him who has feared to pray. You and I would never dare to approach almightiness. But the Almighty, who is humble as well as high and holy (Isa. 57:15), draws very near indeed, and gently lays his hand upon us, and bids us speak to him. Shall we then be so churlish as to refuse?

Here is hope for the transgressor. So which of us is hopeless? If prayer must originate from our own righteousness, who could pray? But prayer begins in the exceeding mercy of him who seeks the lost and who moves our hearts to cry upon him, "God be merciful to me a sinner" (Luke 18:13).

This is why, if a man can breathe, a man can pray. To pray consciously is to breathe more deeply. To pray consciously is to grasp an already extended hand.

II

What Is Prayer Like?

✜✜✜✜✜✜✜✜✜✜✜✜✜✜✜✜✜✜✜✜✜✜✜✜✜✜✜✜✜✜✜✜✜✜✜✜✜

WE HAVE LIKENED PRAYER TO BREATHING. YET PRAYER IN one or other aspect resembles myriad things, while prayer in its entirety defies comparison. For prayer assumes innumerable forms and blesses us in ways beyond our reckoning. Before we examine prayer more closely, let us glance at its multiple variety.

Prayer is simple, like the pebble that a child holds in his hand. But prayer is also formidable, like Mount Everest; and few have gained its summit.

The naturalness of prayer is like the turning of a flower toward the sun. The freedom of prayer is like the ranging of a whale in the ocean. The exaltation of prayer is like the soaring of an eagle above the cloud. The restfulness of prayer is like the quiet of an infant upon his mother's breast.

Prayer is eager, like the heavenward leap of flame. Prayer is mighty, like the fall of heavy waters. Prayer is radiant, like the breaking of the dawn.

Prayer is Adam [1] troubled by God's voice in the garden in the cool of the day (Gen. 3:8). Prayer is the psalmist

[1] Which means Man.

16

rejoicing in the Shepherd's keeping (Ps. 23). Prayer is a dissolute boy coming to himself and turning to his Father (Luke 15:11-20). Prayer is Jesus forgiving from a cross (Luke 23:33-34).

Prayer is entreaty; prayer is acceptance; prayer is a song; prayer is a silence. Prayer is waiting upon God. Prayer is enlisting under that cross.

Prayer is all of these, and more than all of these. Never for long can prayer be one of these alone.

As we investigate various ways of praying we shall discover that certain popular notions of prayer are misconceptions, and that prayer is not so limited a matter as unfamiliarity with it, or even acquaintance with but part of it, might lead one to suppose.

Prayer, for example, to certain men and women, is like a fragile blossom of which the strong winter of our disbelief makes ridicule. But look! In contradiction of our frozen thought prayer again rises from the soul, because the bleakness of our doubt is vanquished by the gentle goodness of the Lord.

To others prayer is like an alphabet to be recited: "This is the way we learned it and this is the way it goes!" But if prayer be no more than recitation of an alphabet, why not recite the alphabet without pretense that we are praying?

Then there are those to whom prayer is like Aladdin's lamp: he who holds this talisman will receive his every wish—regardless! Yet in principle this is unworthy, for it reduces a personal relationship to one that is mechanical or even magical; and, by hoping to subject God to man's whim, it would place man above God. Moreover, it fails in practice: how many of the things we ask are never ours.

In contrast with these limited conceptions we have hinted something of the vastness and diversity of prayer. We shall find that prayer is at once native to us and alien, familiar and incredibly strange. For prayer is like light, "which all men know and which no man knows." Prayer is more homelike than a candle, more sublime than the sun. In as much, therefore, as no man can acquaint himself with prayer except he truly prays, we should be neither hesitant before prayer's lowliness nor presumptuous before its glory. Let us begin where prayer is easiest and most natural, and later press on—it is a lifetime pilgrimage—to larger experience and to knowledge more assured.

III

What Do We Do When We Pray?

❊❊❊❊❊❊❊❊❊❊❊❊❊❊❊❊❊❊❊❊❊❊❊❊❊❊❊❊❊❊❊❊❊❊❊❊❊❊

WHEN WE PRAY WE DO MANY THINGS. SOME OF THESE MAY be evident to persons in our presence, as for example if we kneel or pray aloud. Other acts of prayer may be hidden even from ourself, as when in some worthy cause we concur unwittingly with God, forgetting that it is he who walks and works beside us. Yet probably the largest proportion of our prayer will be known both to God and to ourself, though to no other—as witness the wandering or toiling of our thought, and the posture of our spirit, while we pray. Let us now look more closely at some of these conscious and unconscious elements of prayer.

When we pray, we utter with our lips the cry of our soul.

These words of prayer may be born spontaneously, or they may be spoken from memory, or they may be read from a book, or they may be voiced by another with whom we pray in vocal or in silent unison. But, in one or other manner, the urgent soul is given tongue.

This opening of the soul's prison of silence is the work of articulate prayer. The purpose of such prayer is not to impress the ear but to express the soul's burden. It is not to repeat a required routine but to fling wide upon the mercies of God the closed doors of the spirit. For this reason the true test of words of prayer is neither sound nor authorship nor originality but only effective release of the soul's yearning.

If we have been long without prayer, and would learn to pray, we should probably begin by praying aloud. The central oppression of the soul must be put into words, preferably simple and few, no matter whether they be our own words or those of another adopted as our own.

A naked tailor without cloth, who must straightway go to appear before a king, will borrow the best suit that he can find. Later he may make himself a garment better fitting, but in his need he will not scruple to put on his neighbor's coat.

Just so, when a man must pray, if he be found a naked soul without words, he will at once appropriate the best prayer available. Later, when he has words, he may make himself a new prayer. Meanwhile which prayer is best? Not necessarily the longest or even the smoothest, but that which most readily fits the man when he puts it on. The prayer of the man in Jesus' story which was mentioned earlier has fitted many a man in time of need: "God be merciful to me a sinner" (Luke 18:13).

But we must not stand remote from God, and fling our prayer at heaven, and look to receive mercy in an indifferent heart. We must put on our prayer as personal clothing of the soul, in which we must ourself advance into God's immediate presence, that he may lay his pardoning and renewing hand upon us. Then, when we return to our former place, we shall find it to be a new place, for we ourself shall have been made new.

On the other hand, if we have been long accustomed to pray, we may have formed certain patterns of words which we incline to repeat again and again. Whether such repetition is good or bad depends upon whether it is vital repetition or lazy repetition. Any cook understands this difference. Indeed, who that has ever eaten is ignorant of it?

Vital repetition is exciting. Lazy repetition, on the contrary, is monotonous. Vital repetition prompts the thought, "Oh, good! this again!" But lazy repetition, unless it has already dulled the senses, provokes the murmur, "Oh, no! not this again!" Lazy repetition avoids the new and revolves in a small circle, so that each detail, where there has been change at all, returns again too soon. Vital repetition, however, mingles the new with all of the old, and swings a wide arc in which the familiar is found again with joy. Lazy repetition cramps experience and deadens the spirit; but vital repetition enhances experience and quickens it.

When, therefore, our custom has been to pray in our own words, we should do well to extend the range of our worship by use of a few good books of prayers. We shall wish to mark these books in the margin, and to memorize some of the prayers and to adopt them as our own. For acquaintance with an ever increasing number of worthy prayers can enlarge not only the storehouse of our thought but also our power of devotional expression. Furthermore, it can broaden our understanding of the ways of praying, so that our original prayers become varied and enriched. Certain books of prayers and other helpful writings are listed under "Some Aids to Prayer."

Those of us, moreover, who have grown up in a tradition in which our private prayers as well as the prayers of public worship are contained in the service book of a particular church may find refreshment in occasional resort to other collections of prayers, such as those referred to above. But that worshipful exercise of mind and spirit which may most delight and surprise us may lie first in writing, and then in using, a prayer of our own composition. To be sure, other prayers than ours may be of nobler structure. Yet the cry of our own soul, rising upon wings of our own words, may bring peculiar blessing. Thus we may be encouraged to speak sometimes directly to our Lord, without the intermediate writing.

In the next chapter we shall examine various kinds of spoken prayer. Meanwhile let us turn our attention to other prayerful acts less obvious than speech.

When we pray, we remember and anticipate as under the eyes of God.

This backward and forward extension of the mind, in the midst of prayer, is not, as it appears to be, an interruption. It is rather, as we shall see, part of worship's vital being.

For worship that is alive and strong is like a tree that is nurtured from above by branches reaching into the radiance of God's splendor and the breath of his compassion, and from below by two great roots, which are memory and expectation. Cut off these roots and the tree will wither; and if for sake of sentiment it still be cherished, it will remain a sapless thing, devoid of growth or fruit.

For example, a certain young man raised his thoughts

toward God, and, as it were, saw him, high and lifted up. But straightway into that purity of worship scrambled an impure remembrance: for this young man was a man of unclean lips. Then side-by-side with rag-clad memory crept palsied expectation: for how could an impure man behold God's holiness and live? (Isa. 6:1, 5 ff.)

Suppose now that Isaiah, for this was the name of the young man, had dismissed these two intruders, remembrance and anticipation, and had continued to worship in disregard of them. Then his worship would have become trivial and vain. Then it could never have grappled with his life, and formed it anew, and filled it with power that has blessed the centuries.

To put it otherwise: those memories and expectations that come to us in worship are no mere casual visitors, though they appear to saunter casually, or even irreverently, into the mind. These are memory and expectation with relation to God's holiness. These seemingly intrusive guests have come like the alien Greeks to the feast of the Passover: they "would see Jesus" (John 12:20-21). They have accordingly presented themselves not in disregard of our worship but precisely because of our worship. The holiness of God, in whose presence we stand, penetrating like a bugle call throughout our heart, has summoned all that is within us that would praise him, and all that would beseech his mercy, to assemble openly before his face. And expectation and remembrance have responded.

So we should never turn self-righteously against remembrance and expectancy, to drive them from the temple of prayer. Rather, we should welcome them in strong embrace, and stand with them together before God.

Thus we greet the first remembrance and the first anticipation that step into our thought—and then the next, and the next. Whatever out of yesterday, or out of the day to come, approaches us, whether with uplifted hands of benediction or with a knife to thrust into our ribs, we put our arm about it and hold it close beside us before God. All that so much as peeps out at us from hidden places of awareness we coax into the comprehension of our Father's eyes. With gladness, anxiety, and shame, we range them unreservedly before the face of God. As yet we neither ask nor offer anything: we neither praise nor confess nor implore. We simply bring to the attention of almighty Love those incidents and aspects of the remembered past and of the anticipated future which haunt us in the midst of prayer.

In doing this lies strength. For if recollection or expectancy should be of blessing, then we should be the stronger for binding it to us with bands of gratitude. And if it be of guilt or fear, then we should be the stronger for its healing. The goodness or the wrong which recollection or anticipation brings to mind may, to be sure, seem trivial. Yet to ignore it, is, as we have seen, to render worship itself trivial, and to deceive our own heart. But honestly to deal with it, then and there, before the holy eyes of God, is, in so far, to be made whole.

Jesus, recognizing the urgency of even the small infection of evil that cannot be quarantined from the worshiping mind, pictured a man standing with his gift before the altar of the temple, and there remembering that he had harmed his brother man (Matt. 5:23-24). What then? Should the man dismiss the memory, and pretend that

24

partitioned worship is holy worship, and that an un-cleansed conscience is a worthy conscience? Far otherwise! Deal forthrightly with that memory, Jesus urges; deal with it as under the searching gaze of God: "Leave there thy gift before the altar, and go thy way; first be reconciled to thy brother, and then come and offer thy gift" (Matt. 5:24).

The psalmist, too, found that his mind, in the very midst of brooding upon God, turned backward in recollection and forward in expectancy. "Gracious is the Lord," he cried, "and righteous; yea, our God is merciful. The Lord preserveth the simple" (116:5-6). All *that* is meditation, pure, unmixed. But then remembrance knocked, and was admitted: "I was brought low, and he helped me" (116:6). And then anticipation smiled, and was not turned away: "Return unto thy rest, O my soul; for the Lord hath dealt bountifully with thee" (116:7).

So whenever we seek to worship without remembrance and expectation, we build around ourself a windowless house without doors, from which we cannot escape, and into which we forbid God to come. But when remembrance and expectation are opened before God, they become door-ways of life, through which God walks into our darkness, to shine within our heart, and through which also we walk out with God into the light of a new day.

When we pray, we give gifts to God and we accept gifts at his hand.

This is a free exchange of bestowals, which, daily entered into, makes every day a Christmas of the soul. For that which we thus give to God is not required of us, else it were no gift but an exaction; while that which we receive is beyond our power to purchase or to extort.

But what have we to give to the high and holy God? Nothing, it would seem. Yet God is love (I John 4:16); and that which love yearns to receive is not the same as that which tyranny or greed is eager for. Or turn it around, to look at it from the other side: that which instinctively we give to love is unlike that which we bestow upon covetousness or mere authority. For our offerings to these latter come from without, but that which love distinguishes leaps from within to mingle with external gifts as fire mingles with iron when causing it to glow.

The picture, drawn in miniature, may be seen in family relationship. A child will give from quite outside himself a certain kind of gift to a father who appears to be composed of nothing but money or commandments. But to a father who is the embodiment of wise and understanding love a child will freely render inward offerings which he would never lay before the feet of mere wealth or mere domination.

Let us say that the time of day has come for tucking into bed. There the child-love that is all dependence meets the parent-love which, by comparison, is all wisdom and considerate strength. An exchange of gifts takes place. But what is this that the child gives to the parent? He gives his father his memories and anticipations, compact of glory and gratitude and trouble. And this is the gift which, above all other gifts, a wise and understanding parent craves. For in this meeting of child-love with parent-love it is the yielding of the child's memory and expectation which permits the wisdom and goodness and strength of the parent to become the wisdom and goodness and strength of the child.

What, then, have we to give to the high and holy God? We have our memories and expectations, without bestowal of which all other gifts were poor. That man at the altar, mentioned in the preceding section, therefore hands over to his heavenly Father his memory of selfish pride that separates between him and his brother, together with that memory's accompanying shame. He surrenders also to the Almighty his gleeful or unhappy expectation of meeting his brother in the street while having to avoid his eye; and he gives to God the guilt that accompanies that. Not much of an offering, to be sure! Yet the Lord God wants just such. So he deals with that man not harmfully but cauterizingly. And the man goes out; and not by accident he meets his brother, meets him as though they two were held within a high and holy scrutiny, as indeed they are. Then when the man returns to the temple and again lifts up his face to God, he gratefully recalls a recent cleansing and a yet more recent reconciliation; and expectation touches him with gentle fingers and looks into his eyes, radiant with hope. So the man brings to God this fresh anticipation together with his new remembrance and all the exultation of thanksgiving that bounds within his heart. Then, out of a humble and overflowing spirit, the man presents his material gift, which is no longer merely formal.

When we give to God our memories and expectations, our other gifts to him assume their proper character, and his gifts to us fall into an open and receptive heart. When we give to God our memories and expectations, today becomes truly his. But how can we give today to God until we have given him yesterday and tomorrow?

Let us therefore not assume that yesterday has passed beyond our grasp or beyond the power of God. Look! in our body and in our soul yesterday lives and works today, as present benefit or present woe. What parent has never delighted his child with a tale which he himself had heard in childhood? Or what physician has not been called upon today to minister to yesterday's default?

Nor is tomorrow out of reach, below the visible horizon. Even now, as hope or dread, tomorrow molds our instant thought and deed. Our savings account therefore is made today by expectation of tomorrow's comfort or emergency. And the robber, loitering on the corner, studies the bank, because tomorrow's crime holds him in iron fingers of anticipation.

So when Jesus would bless us, he does it in part by reaching into the past and forgiving our sins, and by reaching into the future and promising peace (Luke 7:48, 50).

It is like a man who was walking down a street when he saw his benefactor and would have turned to join him. But two burly ruffians who had been strolling on either side of the man closed against him, and commanded him to continue with them. So the man was afraid and cried to his benefactor, saying, "Sir, I would walk with you and serve you; but I am helpless between these two men."

The benefactor therefore crossed the street and came to the man, and inquired who his two companions were. And the man replied, "They are the agents of my enemy, an evil man, for whom I once did an evil service. Now they walk with me everywhere and they never let me go."

Then the benefactor questioned the two men as to what their employer paid them. And when they said, "So much," the benefactor promised them much more if they would consent to be washed and clad, and to become his own deputies, to protect this man against his enemy, their former master, and to guard the man's freedom within the benefactor's service. And they agreed. So the man fell upon his knees for joy and said to his benefactor, "Sir, what will you have me do? For my life and all that I have are yours."

Do you ask what street the man was walking? That street is called Today. And the man? He might be you or I. And the two companions? Their names are Memory and Expectation. And the benefactor is Christ, who, if we but open the way by today's prayer, will cross the street, and will come to us wherever we may be, and, redeeming yesterday and tomorrow, will bestow upon us the joyful gift of freedom.

Have we said that a child's gift of memory and expectation is that which a wise and understanding father desires above all other gifts? Perhaps we should have said, Above all gifts but one, which is the gift of the child's self, offered in welcoming the father's love.

Just so, when we accept God's manifold lovingkindnesses, their very acceptance may become the giving of ourself to him, especially as we implant his welcomed love in the fertile center of our life, that it may flourish there and blossom and bear fruit.

When we pray, we express our attitude toward God.
We may do this either intentionally or unawares, as a hungry man, asking his wife about dinner, shows his feeling toward her, whether by conscious word or by unconscious intonation. The man moreover declares his temper by even subtler means, by silent gesture or absence of gesture, by wordless attention or neglect.

Should we then suppose that the Lord God Almighty is less observant than the most jealous wife? As Job well knew (42:2), and the psalmist also, we cannot hide the state of our heart from him who understands our thought afar off (Ps. 139:2). Yet what is this revealing of our attitude toward God but conscious or unconscious prayer?

Such prayer may be the stillness of adoration, merging at its keenest into ecstasy. This latter, to be sure, is not something that we seek. Religious ecstasy is a strong condiment, a single grain or two of which can enliven a great load of mediocrity. It is indeed so very, very good that a little of it may serve a lifetime. For this reason no thoughtful person would try to make a daily meal of it.

But adoration is our common privilege and healthful good. As children know, and they are sometimes wiser than their parents, the privilege of adoration is like the privilege of bread. For adoration nourishes the hungry soul and gives it health. This is why a small child slips into the kitchen while his mother is ironing, and sits in silence on the floor; and when his mother asks him what he wants, replies, "Nothing, I just like to be with you." So the Christian finds himself again and again in the presence of God, wordless, worshipful, adoring, wishing only to be with him whose nearness is blessing upon blessing. This is prayer.

We may, however, express our attitude toward God not only in worshipful adoration but in activity in his behalf, just as children, back from school, learning that their absent mother will be late and tired, get down her cookbook, and beat up a cake all full of eggs. And while these children busy themselves, doing a beautiful thing for their mother, they commune in anticipation with their mother's mind, entering in advance into her joy. Likewise, whenever we do a beautiful thing for God, who is never absent, we truly commune with him, not merely in anticipation, but in immediate relationship; and this communion is either conscious or unconscious prayer.

Again: even in hostility to God we pray; for we cannot stop praying, however much we would. So the question of prayer is not a question of whether we shall pray; it is a question of *how* we shall pray. Here, for example, is a man embittered by the death, twenty-five years ago, of his brother. "I shall never forgive God for that!" he growls, thinking that for a quarter-century no prayer has escaped his heart. Yet on what day has this man not assailed God's ears with all manner of defiance? Antagonism, indeed, is his never ceasing prayer. Hence what would be new to him would be not prayer itself; for he knows that, at least in part, without knowing that he knows it. What would be new to this man would be to pray politely and to be reconciled to God. Then his prayer would win acceptance both with himself and with his Maker, and blessing instead of evil would proceed from it (Jer. 6:19).

It appears, therefore, that the most elementary and the most exalted prayer may be almost equally wordless. For, like human love, communion with God begins and ends in

31

silence; and between these two how-different silences lies the realm of speech. A man at first fails to declare his love for a woman because he loves before he knows that he loves; and at the last, though he has striven manfully with words, he falls again silent before that glory which even highest language can no more contain than a fishing seine can hold a sunrise. Daily, nevertheless, if the man be wise, he struggles with speech; and who shall say that it is unavailing?

It is not otherwise with prayer: for above and below the range of articulate, or even of conscious, worship, like light beyond each end of the visible spectrum, our acts of prayer unbrokenly continue.

When we pray, we join hands with God.

To be sure, since we are creatures of reason, we may most fully co-operate with God when we do so with knowledge and intent. Yet it is possible, after a fashion, to join unknowing hands with him. Since this is not to be despised, let us try to picture it.

A great giant of a man walked on a beach. Beside him stumbled a tiny speck of a child, so little that between the child's uplifted hand and the hand of the man there was a space that was equal, for practical purposes, to infinity. But the space was bridged, because the man held a stick, to the lower end of which five pink fingers clung. Thus the man was able to uphold the child and to guide him. Moreover between father and son there was communion, even while the child's thoughts were on nothing but his own steps, for the father's thoughts were on the child.

Perhaps Jesus had something like this in mind when he emphasized that as we take hold of the familiar end of lowly duties we join hands with God, for God has hold of the other end. It is as though he said, Don't worry overmuch about high things that are beyond your grasp: search your own heart, find where the simple duty lies, do the thing that is right; take hold of that end of the stick, and you will walk right into the kingdom of God (Matt. 25:34-40). "Not every one that saith unto me, Lord, Lord, shall enter into the kingdom of heaven; but he that doeth the will of my Father which is in heaven." (Matt. 7:21.)

Jesus never suggests that we should strive after ecstasies or visions or even the "feeling" of the nearness of God. How down-to-earth his wisdom is! Yet always it is filled with heaven: "Be reconciled to thy brother" (Matt. 5:24); "forgive men their trespasses" (Matt. 6:14); "be merciful" (Luke 6:36); "love one another, as I have loved you" (John 15:12); "he that is faithful in that which is least is faithful also in much" (Luke 16:10). So it happens that in the loyalties of everyday you and I join hands with God by clinging to that homely stick which he has mercifully placed within our grasp; and, though our thoughts may never rise above the stick, or even above our own steps, still, joining hands with God is prayer.

A man, for example, may give himself to the pursuit of beauty, whether of mass or line or color or sound or intellectual abstraction, thinking that there is no God at all, while every day he walks with God, for God has hold of the other end of that stick. And when the man grows up, looks up, and reaches higher, he, who all his life has loved

33

beauty and has sought to serve it, will adore the beauty of his Lord and will worship him in the beauty of holiness. Meanwhile his clinging to that stick is prayer.

Likewise we may devote ourself to truth, while long we fail to understand that God has hold of the other end of that. Yet truth is true because God does have hold of it; and every man who cleaves to truth joins hands with God. Therefore that man who is loyal to truth, despite what he believes to be God's absence, will in immediate relationship keep faith with God, when he looks into his face. Meanwhile he prays unconsciously.

It is so with daily goodness and lovingkindness. No man who has spent himself in love for his fellow men has walked alone. Always God has walked with him, holding the higher end of the stick. To be sure, the man may have ridiculed that which he termed the "supernatural"; he may have thought that he believed in man alone; yet morning after morning he has joined hands with the Lord of life, and thus has prayed.

Indeed, a goodly proportion of the prayer of the saints, also, may be unconscious. For between the saints and these three men just mentioned there may be less difference of heart than either the overpious or the underpious would care to admit.

The distinction, in fact, between the man who glues himself to the stick and the man who consciously joins hands with God, may be primarily less of heart than of dimension and realization. A man with never a thought of Jesus may wear out his life, doing some of the things that Jesus did: for example, healing. This man, to be sure, and his heavenly Father both hold firmly the same stick.

Yet if the man struggles along, believing himself to be fatherless, how vastly poorer his life and influence must be than if he did these things as Jesus did them, in realization of a radiant and empowering comradeship.

For something passes through merged purposes and through like-minded conversation which no stick, however tightly held, is able to communicate. When prayer becomes intentional co-operation with God, life is enlarged in a new direction and enriched with a new quality, like that of an orphan boy who acquires a loving and understanding father whose will it is the boy's delight to do.

When we pray, we meditate upon God's goodness.

A busy man, with a small house on a little plot of land, may tour each day his quarter-acre, noting the beauty and wonder of sprouting seed and opening bud and thickening branch. And this simple, frequent exercise may bear the fruit of quiet thankfulness of mind.

How much more, then, should we be blessed who daily free our thought to investigate the wonderful compassions of God! If we should wish a guide, to help us find our way among the fields and forests and hills and streams of God's manifold mercies, the Bible is full of them, humble and eager and able: the psalmists, the New Testament writers, Jesus himself.

Psalm 23, for example, is just such thinking about God's goodness as we have been speaking of: "The Lord is my shepherd; I shall not [be in] want" (23:1). Psalm 90 ponders the way in which God stands beyond, and yet works through, and puts his arms around, the whole of history and the individual heart: "Lord, thou hast been our dwelling place in all generations. Before the mountains were brought forth, or ever thou hadst formed the earth and the world, even from everlasting to everlasting, thou art God" (90:1-2). In the eighth chapter of Romans, Paul exults in a love that, having found us, leaves us never: "Who shall separate us from the love of Christ? shall tribulation, or distress, or persecution, or famine, or nakedness, or peril, or sword? . . . Nay, in all these things we are more than conquerors through him that loved us" (8:35, 37). And in three short verses of Matthew 10, Jesus broods upon God's care for men and sparrows: "Are not two sparrows sold for a farthing? and one of them shall not fall on the ground without your Father. But the very hairs of your head are all numbered. Fear ye not therefore, ye are of more value than many sparrows" (10:29-31).

Thoughtful and openhearted reflection upon even these few passages should give some hint as to the character of meditative prayer, in which thinking about God's manifold goodness is in a real sense thinking *toward* God; and this turns almost imperceptibly into reaching in God's direction; and this, into acceptance of his outreach toward us.

Thus Psalm 23, opening with meditation upon God's merciful shepherding, concludes in personal resolution: "I will dwell in the house of the Lord for ever" (23:6). And that grand contemplation of God's majesty, beyond, around, and through the processes of history, breaks into joyful realization of God's effective working at our very human finger tips (Ps. 90:17). And Jesus, seeing a sparrow rest upon God's arm, finds fear dethroned (Matt. 10:31).

And Paul, marveling before the exceeding brightness of Christ's love, turns his dazzled eyes within, and knows himself made more than conqueror through him who loved him (Rom. 8:37).

All these things, and vastly more, our guides can bring to our attention. Again and again the wise will journey with them into these highlands that they know so well. The timid, perhaps, may never leave their side. If we be bold, however, we shall observe not only all that our guides can show us of the landscape but also their principles of exploration, until we ourself shall be able to wander freely in the kingdom of God.

Yet when we venture "on our own," we shall do as children of the city do who "hike" in the country: we shall beg a ride out of our overcrowded thoughts before we begin to walk. Perhaps we shall encounter one of our familiar guides returning to his home among the crags and peaks. Or we may climb into such hospitable conveyance as comes along: Augustine's *Confessions;* or à Kempis' *Imitation of Christ;* or Luther's triumphant affirmation, *"A Mighty Fortress Is Our God";* or the recollection of that light, unquenched beneath a spate of tears, which once we saw within a childless mother's face, defying the elemental waters like a beacon in a hurricane. And we shall find ourself transported out of our dusty-mindedness, and a voice, as it were, will sound within us, "You are now in God's domain; there is the path to those mountains." And we shall set off alone, though not in loneliness, and great will be our joy.

We shall let our thought run free, like a happy child investigating a new estate. We shall gaze upon the goodness of God, in length and breadth and depth and height. We shall pick such blossoms as invite us, and we shall gather treasure from the unspoiled hills. We shall enlarge our soul among vistas of the infinite. We shall note paths later to be explored and springs to which we shall return.

And the living Spirit of Christ, greater than any mortal guide, psalmist, apostle, or even earthly Jesus, shall walk with us, leading us into new truth (John 16:13). For one of the offices of meditative prayer is to free us in his company for just such fresh discovery.

When we pray, we listen, that we may heed the voice of God.[1]

The whole Bible tingles with this twofold fact of prayer: that we may speak directly to God and that God speaks directly to us. Prayers, accordingly, are made after the manner of conversation—which is to say, not only with our lips but with our ears.

What hope, indeed, should we hold for an invalid who would pray to his physician only with his mouth and would turn away before the man of healing had spoken? Or what judgment should we pronounce upon a soldier who would freely speak but would never listen while in the presence of his commanding officer? Or what future should we suppose to await a child who in all things would instruct his parent, but would himself be instructed in nothing? Yet is it otherwise between ourself and our Father who is in heaven?

---

[1] In this section we are concerned with the open ear which welcomes God's voice. But God does not speak upon our command. Therefore, in Chapter VII we consider "prayer in perplexity."

So when we pray, we both speak and harken. We attune our inward ears to the secret whisper of God. Like parched land opening its crevices for rain, like a compassless and cloud-enshrouded mariner searching for the sun, like a returning lover straining to catch across the garden wall the dear accent of his beloved, the soul bends every faculty to welcome the interior command of God, which brings at once the quenching of the soul's thirst, a sure hand upon life's unsure helm, and sweetest consolation.

But how shall we know the voice of God, and to what shall it be likened? It may be likened to whatever bears its own unquestionable witness, needing none to cry concerning it, "Lo! here," or "Lo! there" (Matt. 24:23) . For when the word of God vibrates within our soul, straightway we know it for what it is, as we know the breaking of day or the stirring of love or the summons of death.

To be sure, in advance of the event we may debate and misunderstand, as a man at midnight may insist that a street lamp is the uplifting sun. Yet when, above the dark horizon, swings the source of all our earthly lamps, down-pouring its radiance until the very alleys are filled and every field is flooded with light, what man among us with open eyes would then maintain that only that thing shines which human hands have fashioned on a pole? We should then know that this is in truth the day, but we should know simply because the self-witnessing event has come.

Here, however, is a man who misconstrues as a decree from heaven the echo of his own stubbornness. Does this disprove that God communicates his will to us? Only to those eager for such disproof. To others it might merely mean that dusty-mindedness has once again forejudged the event. Forejudged it; therefore judged it falsely, not proved it false. This misjudging man, like that other man just mentioned, has confused man's devising with God's bestowal. He has not shown that God does not bestow.

When, moreover, the fields and alleys of the mind are visited by Light needing no further testimony than itself; when, in the depths, our soul is shaken by an unequivocal Voice, not overwhelming us like thunder, but at once abasing and exalting us through the gentleness of unquestionable authority, like the authority of springtime—then debate and misunderstanding wilt in shame, and we are left confronting the ultimate fact: to obey this Voice we were born. Hence the Scripture cries and cries again:

> Today, when you hear his voice,
> do not harden your hearts.
> —Heb. 3:7, 15; 4:7 R.S.V.

IV

What Shall We Say in Prayer?

✸✸✸✸✸✸✸✸✸✸✸✸✸✸✸✸✸✸✸✸✸✸✸✸✸✸✸✸✸✸

WHEN WE PRAY, THERE MAY BE ONE THING ONLY THAT WE wish to say, perhaps but one word, "God." Or thoughts may jostle one another to be uttered, like children crushed in the gateway of a carnival.

In this latter case, as with children wedging an entrance, our thoughts would benefit by being gently brought to order. Likewise, in opposite extreme, if our prayer consists of a single word, unless our state be indeed exceptional, ordered extension of the range of prayer should bring joyful reward. Let us therefore try to understand something of the forms of spoken prayer. In Chapter VII we shall look at spoken prayer in relation to varied circumstance. Here let us consider ways in which the worshiping mind speaks.

When we pray, we shall ask something for ourself.
This is called petition.

Petition may be the first prayer of infant lips and the last prayer of old age. It may indeed be the only prayer that we know. Even the solitary word "God," fervently uttered, is petition at its briefest, meaning, "God help me."

So natural and so universal is petition that probably this is that of which most persons think whenever the word "prayer" is mentioned. For without petition we should hardly pray at all.

Petition may be selfish or almost wholly selfless. It may be like the howl of a spoiled baby or like the request of a soldier to be sent on a certain urgent mission involving probable death. But we shall not nervously debilitate ourself, analyzing the selfishness or unselfishness of our petitions. We shall forthrightly offer such petitions as heart and mind press upon our lips. Then if we can find it in us to do so, we shall pray that, both without and within, God may have his way with us; and that our prayers, wherever they have been amiss, may be forgiven; and, wherever right, may be confirmed. Then, without fret as to whether our prayers have been selfish or otherwise, we shall do the next necessary thing.

We shall ask forgiveness, also, for whatever has been wrong, whether known or unknown, in our deed or thought or heart. If we should think that there has been no wrong in us, then much indeed would be wrong (I John 1:8-9). So we shall pray not only to be forgiven but to be strengthened to accept God's pardon without reserve, that we may build it into the daily structure of our life, as bricks are built into the side of a house.

We shall pray, accordingly, that we may daily become more forgiving toward our fellow men. And we shall pray with special reference to any person whom we find it difficult or almost impossible to forgive. For forgiveness is all of one piece: how shall we accept it from God unless we expend it upon men? or how shall we give it to men except we receive it from above? Jesus underscored this, insisting that to be unforgiving and unforgiven is the same, and that the heart needs to be filled brimful with forgivingness and forgiven-ness (Matt. 6:14-15; 18:21-35).

All of which is to say that we shall seek, through petition, the cleansing of the heart. For the pure in heart see God (Matt. 5:8), but to the evil heart nothing is good. Therefore one of God's most precious blessings is the gift of a clean heart and clear eyes (Matt. 6:22, 23). These may be had for the asking, though hardly in any other way. For a prudish heart is not clean, and a haughty eye is not clear. Yet if a man, with the broom of his own will, sweep from his heart so much as one-tenth of the evil that is native there, how shall he prevent self-righteousness from stealing in to sit in the same chair where earlier evil sat? (Matt. 12:43-45.) But to be cleansed as God cleanses, a heart must be both emptied and filled. It must be freed of the coarse sins of "evil" men and of the refined sins of "good" men, vanity and greed and bitterness and envy.

Then it must be filled with the gracious oil of humility, and set aflame with the love that is in Christ. Thus the spirit of a man becomes, in a dark and hopeless world, the hopeful candle of the Lord (Prov. 20:27; Matt. 5: 14-16). This may be ours for the asking. But when it is given to us, we shall be unaware of it. So we shall continue to ask, and we shall continue to receive. And when thereby the world about us shall be blessed, we shall marvel greatly, not knowing how that blessing comes.

In our petitions, then, we shall pray for whatever we need: for work and bread and clothing; for enlargement of

43

mind; for enrichment of heart; for strength and patience; for healing and guidance. Especially we shall implore those gifts which are essential if the life that is in Christ is to become the life that is in ourself. We shall not hesitate, as Paul reminded certain early Christians, to seek the best gifts of heart and mind (I Cor. 12:31—13:13). These indeed are they which God most eagerly bestows (Luke 11:9-13). So how pitiful it would be, merely for want of ambition, to lack forever life's richest gain! Yet many are poor because they never greatly pray (Matt. 13:44).

When we pray, we shall ask something for another. This is called intercession.

If ever we have prayed in behalf of a loved one, intercession is in so far familiar. Yet perhaps something of its wider sweep and power remains to be explored. Two pictures may help to illustrate this.

A certain man believed in neither God nor men: he was without faith. This man was also without love: he cared for no one but himself, and himself he despised. This man was likewise devoid of hope: he had entered into every pleasure and had found it empty; he had tasted every evil and he could not wash the bitterness of it out of his mouth. Moreover, this man was minus integrity: being true to nothing, he had played false even with his own soul.

The question arises, What was this man worth? Does it matter that he was the wealthy and powerful ruler of a wealthy and powerful nation? Or does this raise the further question, If king and people were alike, what would be the value of that nation? Is not the answer in both instances the same: that that man or that nation would have little

44

worth indeed, apart from the possibility of attaining integrity and faith and hope and love?

But here is another Man. He is slowly dying, stretched upon a cross of wood. His faith in man, as man is visited by the Spirit of God, has strengthened multitudes of bent and burdened men to stand erect. His trust in God has quickened the fainting soul and has brought gracious light to eyes that were darkened. His timeless hope, embracing the world and encompassing heaven, has opened a gate upon immortality for men and women imprisoned in dust. His love, cascading as a river from the cross, has made gardens in our desert. And this Man's dying with the integrity of his soul intact has put a core of iron into the spirit of his friends. Is not this Man worth everything it costs to make his Spirit our own?

At some movable point between these two men most of us pass our days. We are not without faith, yet such faith as we possess is sometimes more like stilts on which we precariously balance than like living rock on which our being is based. We are not unloving, yet our love is perhaps as often a trickle as a torrent; a flicker, as often as a blaze of light. A handful of hope most of us hold, until the world knocks against us and the hope is lost. But how rare and enviable is a soul that is filled with hope which the world cannot spill! Integrity? We know the meaning of that, according to our measure. Yet the full implication of integrity is perhaps hidden from us until we look at the Christian symbol. This is formed by a will reaching upward toward God, across which the will of the world horizontally strikes. But if integrity can have free course only from a cross, it still may be more precious than diamonds.

Now: in view of these two pictures and of ourself between them, what is the best that we could wish for our loved ones, for our friends, for our world? We could wish that they might dwell in material comfort, yet hardly at the cost of fullness of life: the king in our story existed in material comfort, but, within his still perambulating flesh, the man was dead. Again, we could wish that loved ones might be spared pain and sorrow, yet scarcely at the cost of wealth of being and greatness of heart: perhaps such joy as grief can only enrich and such peace as pain can only deepen would be even better than suffering's absence. So, on and on. Wherever we penetrate beneath the show of things, we find that the best that we could wish for anyone is all compressed in Christ. "In him was life; and the life was the light of men." (John 1:4.)

Intercession accordingly is at its best when it makes its own the wisdom that is in Jesus, and pleads in his Spirit. Then it seeks in behalf of family, or friend, or even enemy, the highest gifts which heaven can bestow.

Yes, intercession at its apex includes the enemy. Perhaps the real meaning and force of intercession must be withheld from us until we have prayed from the heart in behalf of one whom we despise or actively hate. Was not this what Jesus did from the cross! "Father, forgive them; for they know not what they do." (Luke 23:34.) Thus he fulfilled his own commandment, "Pray for them which despitefully use you, and persecute you" (Matt. 5:44). So it *can* be done! And when it is done repeatedly by anyone, in humble sincerity, how shall God fail, round about those prayers, to purge hatred away and to change the climate of life and to cause a new spirit to bloom?

46

When we pray, we shall give thanks to God.

But if someone says, "What have I to be thankful for?" the answer may be other than expected. For one anticipates the familiar provocation to argument, "You have so many blessings, why don't you count them?" Yet the true answer may be, "What, indeed, if the essential thing be lacking?"

It is like a man born blind, who in the midst of daylight railed at darkness. When his friends said to him, "You should be thankful for the beauty of this world," he replied, "Beauty? Where is beauty? I see no beauty!" But a physician touched the man's eyes and the man saw. Then the man's heart overflowed in daily thankfulness for the skill and gentleness of his physician, and for the light of the sun, and the clouds of the sky, and the trees of the field, and the faces of his friends.

Again, it is like a man who on a rainy night slipped and fell in front of a speeding automobile. But the automobile passed over the man, leaving him unharmed. So he arose and returned safely home. When the dawn came, and the man went out of his house and looked upon the day, he saw, as one reborn, all things made new. For he said to himself, "I should be dead; but I am alive!" Therefore a drink of cold water, or the softness of grass beneath the man's feet, filled him with rapture. Thus he became thankful for much for which he would not previously have offered praise.

What have we to be thankful for? What, indeed, if the essential thing be absent, for want of which our eyes are darkened and our soul is dulled? Many a man must receive from God one thing more than he has yet received, before his heart will be at all disposed to thankfulness. But then he will give thanks in all things (I Thess. 5:18) .

Hence the exceeding joyfulness of the gospel of forgiveness. For when the night of unforgiven-ness is lifted from the soul, and a man sees all things clearly in God's light, shall he not then abound in praise and exultation? And when, within a man, the spirit has been numb and dull, to point of deadness, but now with glad wonder the man finds himself, under the touch of Christ, alive and sensitive to blessing, what that the world can do to him can stop his thankful adoration? For the essential thing has now been given him, by which all other gifts are known (I Cor. 2:12) , and by which the climate of the soul is changed from thanklessness to gratitude.

Then the man may call the roll of his blessings, though this may not be quickly finished. It may go on from dawn until dark, from dark until sleep. For as a man advances in Christian experience and understanding, thanksgiving occupies ever larger proportion of his prayer.

Listen to Paul, writing from prison to beloved friends who faced grievous peril: "Rejoice in the Lord always: again I will say, Rejoice. . . . In nothing be anxious; but in everything by prayer and supplication with thanksgiving let your requests be made known unto God. And the peace of God, which passeth all understanding, shall guard your hearts and your thoughts in Christ Jesus" (Phil. 4:4, 6-7 A.S.V.) .

If any man thinks that Paul was indulging a luxurious fancy, this man should move over to make room in his life for Christ. Then this man, too, could know the secret of thanksgiving.

When we pray, we shall confess our sins.

However, if we be unaware of sin, we shall surely not confess it. For falsely to confess would be not to make confession but to make falsehood. And if falsehood be ever justified, it is not so in prayer, which is response of the truth within us to the Truth which is God. Therefore when we pretend in prayer, we merely put on a sideshow[1] by which God is neither deceived nor amused.

Likewise we shall not try to work up a "feeling" of sinfulness. Such feeling, artificially induced, would itself be artificial. Nor is there virtue in such feeling, even when it is genuine.

That which we shall daily strive to do, with all strength and perseverance, is to expose ourself, exactly as we are, whether in Freudian sense or in common sense, to God as he is found in Christ, who walks the pages of the Gospels[2] and stirs the highest prompting of our heart.

In the Gospels, to be sure, are certain perplexities. But these are relatively few. If we be wise, we shall place them upon a shelf marked "for future consideration." Then as we acquire Christian experience and knowledge, by which to interpret them, we shall, if they still seem important to us, review them. And if need be, we shall later review them again. But the importance of the Gospels is not in what we do not understand. The importance of the Gospels lies in that which grasps our conscience and moves our spirit

---

[1] Jesus' word, "hypocrite," means literally, "play-actor." See Matt. 6:5, and elsewhere.

[2] The first four books of the New Testament: Matthew, Mark, Luke, and John.

until we cannot avoid understanding. And of this present power there is abundance in those pages.

In due course, then, as we are laid hold of by the simple force of the Gospels, a dual awareness is likely to form within us: that if God were like Jesus, we should be deeply satisfied; and that if we were like Jesus, God would have reason to be satisfied with us. Then one more momentous step: God *is* like Jesus (John 14:9; II Cor. 4:6) ; and God is grievously and eternally unsatisfied with less in us than the Spirit which was in his Son (Col. 1:9-13, 27-28). The contrast, then, between our own spirit and the Spirit of Christ is the measure of our sin.

Therefore, although a man may think himself to be a fine fellow, and no sinner, when measured by his own standards or even by the standards of his family and friends, still, when he gazes hard at Christ, he may decide that deep within himself he is all but destitute of that essential quality of being which God requires of him, and in which Christ is measurelessly rich, and which he himself must gain before his life can become whole.

In homely phrase it is like a young man in medical school, who took his studies lightly and was content with a minimum of work, until one morning when a famous surgeon performed an operation before that student's eyes. Then the young man was filled with shame and with unquenchable desire, and he said to himself, "I must learn to operate like that, though it takes my life to do it!"

Sin, this is to say, is failure of spirit which is brought to awareness by the presence of perfection. Christ is the way (John 14:6) ; sin is that insufficiency of spirit which falls by the wayside. Christ is the mark at which the Christian aims his life (Eph. 4:13) ; sin is that unsteadiness of spirit which misses the mark. Christ is the Christian's law (Rom. 8:2) ; sin is that lawlessness of spirit which lives in disregard of Christ. Christ is righteousness (I Cor. 1:30) ; sin is that self-centeredness of spirit which is the essence of unrighteousness, even when it is self-righteousness.

These four words, "falling-by-the-wayside," "missing-the-mark," "lawlessness," "unrighteousness," recur in the Greek of the New Testament again and again. The first two of them are generally translated by the English word "sin." But all four words represent a spirit that fails to measure up to God's design for us as known in Christ.

To what shall we liken this? Sin, we may say, is a fig tree that is without figs. Or again, sin is an eagle whose wings remain untried, because he creeps throughout his life along the ground. Or yet again, sin is a human soul that has been made a nesting place of scorpions. For the soul was meant to be filled with a pure and purifying love, like the love that is in Jesus (John 15:12) . The soul was meant to spread strong wings of faith and to rejoice before the very face of God (Rom. 5:1-5) . The soul was meant to bear abundant fruit of kindliness, like the kindliness of our Father who is in heaven (John 15:8; Luke 6:36) . In so much, therefore, as we be barren of the fruits of mercy; in so much as we be earth-bound; in so much as there be venom or uncleanness in us—we have sinned. For we have failed in that for which we were designed.

Thus many a man, when the glory of Christ has burst upon him, has been moved with shame because of his default and with new resolve because of the boundless claim and hope of Jesus (Matt. 5:48) . Then confession has

51

followed, not as brooding upon inferiority, but as the healthful cleansing of the heart; not as turning back toward old shadows, but as advancing into the light; not as bewailing bondage, but as the casting off of bonds.

Then the seeming contradiction between the Christian's daily petition for strength and daily confession of sin is resolved as a man's understanding of Christ deepens and widens, revealing not only Christ's presence and power but also new areas of thought and of experience to be brought under Christ's control. It is like a man starting to walk to a distant mountain, who after many a dusty hour sees that the object of his striving is still farther away than it appeared to be when he set out in its direction. To those, however, who are acquainted with the deceptiveness of mountain distances this man's admission, that despite his toiling he seems no nearer to his goal, is more convincing of real progress than is the easy brag of some loiterer, "Oh, that mountain? I could walk to that easily enough, if I wanted to!" For realization of the mountain's true remoteness comes only to him who advances toward it.

Thus the more a man knows of Christ, the more keenly he is aware that as yet he is possessed of Christ only in part. So there is daily petition for strength and there is daily confession of sin. Then as the man increases in Christian comprehension and in Christian life, his confession grows not less but greater, both in depth and in breadth, until it embraces the whole body of mankind, of which the man knows himself to be an inseparable part. Then the sin of mankind is seen as his sin, and the need of mankind becomes his daily burden. So in this man's prayer confession matches intercession, reaching out long arms of yearning that envelop the world.[3]

When we pray, we shall entrust ourself and our loved ones to God's keeping. This is called commitment or commendation.

In such commitment lies the calm security, the ease of heart, and the peaceful joy of the Christian life. This is part of that "blessedness" of which Jesus spoke in the Beatitudes, a word which means literally "blessedly happy" (Matt. 5:3-12) . This stands in contrast with the insecure and unblessed happiness which is the best that the world can give to us as long as we turn our face away from the face of the Father. For the happiness that is of the world is always unstable and anxious: it collapses, and knows in advance that it must collapse, before the malice of an enemy, or the failure of a friend, or the changing wind of circumstance, or the closing gate of the years.

The happiness that is of the world is like a certain slave who eluded his master and masqueraded as a king: aware that his falsehood could not long be hidden, he plunged desperately into every proffered luxury and excitement. But the "blessed happiness" of the children of God is like a king who adopted the raiment of his subjects and walked among them, doing good, secure in his possession of the kingdom, assured that the day of his revealing would be a day of gladness (Phil. 2:3-11; Rom. 8:19) .

This word meaning "blessedly happy" was used by the

[3] Readers familiar with my *Prayers of the Christian Life* will recognize in this section an enlargement of the brief statement heading the prayers of confession in that book.

early Greeks to describe the imagined condition of their gods upon Olympus. But Jesus boldly applies this word to any man in the street who follows in his steps. It is but varied application of his assurance to the eleven,[4] "These things have I spoken unto you, that in me ye might have peace. In the world ye shall have tribulation: but be of good cheer; I have overcome the world" (John 16:33).

Here then is peace dependent not upon absence of trouble but upon assured victory over trouble (Rom. 8:37). Here is joy springing not from fulfillment of our own will, which is always in some respect, and often in most respects, defective; but here is joy that springs from daily dwelling within the will of God, which is forever perfect (Rom. 12:2). Here is true security, for nothing occurs that is beyond the range of that Authority by which our days are kept, whether "life, or death, or things present, or things to come" (I Cor. 3:22).

So we no more require that our sea be smooth than does the little eider duck that confidently rides the stormy wave. It is not essential that our self-made plans be brought to pass; it is essential that our hearts be kept in the embrace of Love that is all-wise and never-failing. For by Love our wounds are healed (Isa. 53:5; 30:26), our grief is comforted (Isa. 51:12), our crooked places are made straight (Isa. 40:4), and every bitter thing is turned to blessing (Heb. 12:11). This is the salvation of God. This the psalmist had experienced who prayed, "I will fear no evil: for thou art with me" (23:4). This is the unassailable stronghold of the saints, which may be also ours: "If God

---

[4] One of the twelve, Judas Iscariot, was not present.

be for us," beyond, within, and round about, our every day, "who can be against us?" (Rom. 8:31.)

So we commend ourself to God, believing that in only superficial sense can we ourself protect ourself, but joyfully persuaded that only with salutary power can trouble come to us while we remain within God's leading and defense (Rom. 8:28; 5:3-5).

V

When Shall We Pray?

THERE IS, AS ANY GARDENER KNOWS, A SEASON FOR THE planting of each special seed. Prayer likewise has its seasons, which we who would learn to pray must learn to honor. This is not to say that we may not pray at any time. It is to say that in the healthful Christian life there are times for planting and times for reaping, and that he who prays only in rare emergency handicaps God by not having prayed in season.

It is like a man in a northern state who owned a dozen apple trees. This man ate fruit which fell to the ground, but he never picked fruit at the time for picking. Neither did he loosen or enrich the earth, or prune the branches, or spray the forming fruit. Neither did he plant, against the failure of this aging orchard.

Yet when a February gale descended and all his trees, groaning with ice, were destroyed, this man seized a pickax and rushed from his house into the storm. He chipped twelve holes in the resisting ground. Then in each hole he placed a long-dried apple seed.

Do not ask whether those seeds grew! In God's mercy things wonderfully and undeservedly occur. But ask whether this man's example is to be followed, either in the raising of fruit or in the cultivation of prayer.

Only let him who would condemn this man beware, lest thereby he condemn himself. For who has not failed to nurture prayer in season? Who has not neglected planting until destruction fell? Who has not, too late, chipped a desperate niche in his frozen heart for prayer? Yet through God's mercy, even so, we have been wonderfully and undeservedly rewarded.

Prayer at its effective best, however, is co-operation with God, not imposition upon him. The praying man disciplines himself to reverence the will of God and the seasons of the soul. Hence the question, When shall we pray?

We shall pray each night, shortly before falling asleep.

Thus the soul prepares for rest. Thus the way is opened for God to visit us with secret restoration (Ps. 23:3).

What father, roughing it with his young son, will refuse, when evening comes, to help the boy remove his tangled pack? Will he not gladly free the boy's bonds, and lift aside his load, and do his utmost for the lad, that he may sleep and be refreshed? How much more, then, shall our heavenly Father stoop to us in our evening prayer, and free us from the weight that heavily oppresses, and minister with healing carefulness to our repose?

Hence the prayer of the psalmist, "I will both lay me down in peace, and sleep: for thou, Lord, only makest me dwell in safety" (4:8). And again, "Cast thy burden upon the Lord, and he shall sustain thee" (Ps. 55:22). And yet again, the gracious word of Jesus, "Come unto me, all ye that labour and are heavy laden, and I will give you rest" (Matt. 11:28). And still again, the quiet voice of Jesus' follower, "Casting all your care upon him; for he careth for you" (I Pet. 5:7).

Evening prayer, accordingly, seeks not to equip oneself for toil or conflict but to make ready for rest. It is not the gathering up of resources; it is the laying aside of care. It is primarily prayer of disburdenment.

Therefore whatever the burden of our heart, we name it. Moreover, we commend that burden to God's mercy and power. Then we name the next burden and do likewise with it—and the next and the next. Thus we touch, each for a moment, with fingers that are glad or grieved or shamed or anxious, the varied cargo of our heart.

So evening prayer embodies thanksgiving. For who, that has lived for a whole day in the keeping of God, must not, when evening comes, turn to him freighted with praise? (Ps. 103:1.) In glad and forthright words, accordingly, we render thanks for all the mercies of God's care, and we commend to his wise providence those things in which our joy consists.

Is there also burden of shame? We confess it in plain, ungilded words, beseeching pardon. Then we commend that sin to God. Which is to say, like a little child on whose arm a tarantula clings, we hold it out to our Father, imploring him to take it away. How long in such case shall we have to plead? Are we to suppose that God will bide his time and that he will not straightway save us? Will he not, rather, before our first cry has become mute in our own ears, reach forth his hand and remove our sin far from us? (Isa. 65:24; Ps. 103:10-14.)

Or is there burden of sorrow? Then we unlatch grief's closed door, to admit "the Father of mercies, and the God of all comfort" (II Cor. 1:3). We must not keep our grief sealed up, else it will sour and spread its poison of bitterness through all the secret channels of life. In Chapter VII more will be said of prayer in sorrow. Enough for now that in our evening prayer we frankly utter our complaint, as it is written, "Pour out your heart before him" (Ps. 62:8). Into grief's unlighted chamber we usher the shining Lord of life. There we make known to him its emptiness and darkness. Yet suddenly it is no more empty, for he is there. It is no longer dark, for he has lightened it. The joy of our Lord has become our joy, deeper than human loneliness, stronger than human sorrow. For the angel of the Lord's presence has rolled away the burden of our grief, like that great stone that sealed the tomb of Jesus (Matt. 27:66—28:2); and there is triumph. And there is rest.

Or are we burdened by anxiety? It is not God's will that his children should be anxious (II Tim. 1:7). For anxiety is the special privilege of those who ignore the claim of God upon them or the care of God for them.

But when a man places himself under God's rule, he takes his stand within God's protection. Moreover, if our dog, while walking with us, is emboldened by our human presence, so as to challenge enemies larger than he by many times, how much more should we ourself be freed from fear who take no step apart from God. Indeed the very same anxiety which, in forgetfulness of God, seems only wise, appears, when we stand beneath God's arm to look at it, almost silly. Hence Jesus, who was ever mindful of God, was astonished because of the fear of his disciples, who had forgotten God, when they and Jesus were together in the selfsame storm: "Why are ye fearful, O ye of little faith?" (Matt. 8:26.)

So, in our evening prayer, concealing nothing, we tell our God our whole fear. Next, we give him charge of it and of ourself. Into his faithful keeping, who never slumbers nor sleeps (Ps. 121:4), we commend ourself, our loved ones, and all our concerns. Then, like a little child in his father's arms, we lay down our head, and rest, as it is written, "When thou liest down, thou shalt not be afraid: yea, thou shalt lie down, and thy sleep shall be sweet" (Prov. 3:24).

Thus evening prayer includes all of those acts of private worship which have been mentioned earlier[1]: the giving of thanks, the confession of sins, the cry for help, the pleading in behalf of others, the resting of care upon "the everlasting arms" (Deut. 33:27). To be sure, from evening to evening the proportion of these elements will vary. Today there may be more detailed thanksgiving, tomorrow more extensive intercession. Yet, almost without exception, those five just-named ingredients, however briefly voiced, belong to evening prayer.

But, throughout all, the emphasis falls upon commitment. Evening confession, as we have seen, is of one piece with that; for as we acknowledge our sins, we yield ourself anew to God's Holy Spirit. Nor can evening praise be parted from commitment; for in it we bring an offering of ourself to God. Evening petition and intercession, likewise, are the petition and intercession of commitment; for

[1] In Chapter IV.

60

as we pray in our own behalf and in behalf of others, we return again with them into the garrison of God's defense.

So all of the elements of evening prayer minister to repose, and all of them together form one prayer of restful commitment, as wood and steel and cotton and wool make one warm bed in which a man lies down to sleep.

We shall pray each morning, shortly after awakening.

As compared with evening prayer this is like a man arising from sleep and throwing aside his blanket and putting on his suit. For although both be made of the same substance, a man will neither wear his suit to bed nor his blanket to work. For the one is designed for rest, but the other for labor.

Morning prayer, likewise, although it may embody the same elements as evening prayer, is differently put together and differently employed. Here is not the casting aside of burdens; here is the girding of the loins for toil. Here is not the quieting of thought; here is kindling of the mind. Here is not preparation for rest; here is provision for achievement.

Morning prayer begins with thanksgiving. For who that has tasted the goodness of the Lord (Ps. 34:8) can at any time address him with praiseless lips?

Morning prayer continues in petition that the will of God may be known and done, both in the world at large and in our own endeavor. A man who thus comes to his day, with thankfulness and with co-operation in the will of God, is like a man on a mountain top, whose task is to dislodge a boulder that will then take itself into the valley where it is needed.

But a man who begins his day dejected, because he disdains the mercies of God, and who comes willfully to a willful task, because he disregards God's will—this man is like one who digs a great rock from a ravine and, bending himself beneath its weight, bears it upon his shoulders up the reluctant slope.

In morning prayer, accordingly, we review our plans and problems before the face of Christ. We let him shine upon them, and we judge them in his shining. Thus we inquire the mind of Christ concerning them. Then when we take our tasks in hand, we try to work things out in the light of that revealing. For Christ makes his own light and sheds it freely before the feet of those who walk with him (John 12:46). But the man of willful mind makes his own darkness and stumbles, enshrouded in that, wherever he goes (Matt. 6:23).

Thus morning prayer includes commitment. This, however, differs from the commitment of evening prayer as the trust of a child in his father's arms differs from the trust of a soldier in his commanding officer. For the one is commitment that results in rest, whereas the other is commitment that results in action.

Yet Christ not only shines authoritatively upon his disciple's path; he furthermore dwells energizingly within his disciple's heart. He who stood by the apostle Paul and said to him, "My grace is sufficient for thee: for my strength is made perfect in weakness" (II Cor. 12:9), forsakes not one of his own. Hence morning prayer includes acceptance of the indwelling Spirit of Christ, enabling each of us for that which he commands, until we can rejoice as Paul rejoiced, "I can do all things through Christ which strengtheneth me" (Phil. 4:13) .

Intercession also has place in morning prayer, as does other voicing of concern or need.

There is not time for this? Such prayer, including all its parts, need not be lengthy. A man finds time to eat his breakfast, because neglect of proper nourishment takes toll in weakened flesh. Shall we not likewise feed the soul and strengthen it by morning prayer, lest we confront the day with spirit unequal to its challenge?

Time may be found, if nowhere else, by waking five or ten or fifteen minutes earlier. Then that brief unhurried interval may be filled with prayer. As for those lost few minutes of extra sleep, the resoration that occurs in worship is abundant recompense, like that measureful of borrowed grain, mentioned in the Gospels, which is returned to one "pressed down, and shaken together, and running over" (Luke 6:38) .

Morning prayer, moreover, need not be limited to that one period. When a man wishes to pray, occasion is found. It would be hard, for example, to prevent a man who wanted to do so from praying while bathing or while drinking his coffee or while walking or riding to work.

When Jesus condemned the Pharisees for praying on street corners (Matt. 6:5) , his anger was directed not against an act of worship but against self-righteous display of it—a temptation to which, in exactly that form, a twentieth-century American male is perhaps unlikely to succumb. But it is not impossible, standing with a dozen other persons at a bus stop, to retire into the closet of our mind, and there to commune in secret with him who seeth in secret (Matt. 6:6), while our eyes remain wide open and our hands rest in our pockets.

We shall pray at midday in secret inwardness of worship.

Manifestly such prayer, like many another, may be offered in silence from office desk or drugstore counter or wherever we may be. Often, however, in large cities, churches are open throughout the day. There one may slip quietly into a pew, removed from disturbances of street or of place of business, for that restoration which is ours through prayer.

Perhaps, however, the thought of prayer at midday is so strange as to be unwelcome. Indeed to me it once seemed as odd as that. "Surely," I said to myself, "to pray at noon is carrying a good thing too far. Prayer at night," I continued, "is no doubt valuable. Even prayer in the morning may have its place. But who would wish to tangle his whole day in a cat's cradle of religious routine?"

Clearly the germ of truth in such thinking lies in that familiar word "routine." For if prayer at any time be mere routine, it might better be left unspoken. Certainly routine prayer may be as far from vitalizing as a routine kiss, and quite as hypocritical, and even more of a nuisance. But who that is in love would tell us that a kiss must be only a lame repetition of a lame repetition? One who is in love would scorn such words. He would speak, instead, of shooting stars and of lightning in the veins. In this he would speak truly, telling us not about routine but about the kiss of lovers.

Then what of prayer at midday that is no more routine

than the pressing of parched lips into a bubbling spring, though daily the man pass that way and daily pause to quench his thirst at the waters of life? (Rev. 22:17.) Such repetition could hardly qualify as mere routine. Rather, it would be the essential reviving of one's being. Mere routine would begin when a man would bow himself above the spring without drinking, or when he would daily lower his face into a dried channel after the spring had ceased to flow. But our God is a fountain that never fails to satisfy us, so long as we ourself fail not to thrust our mouth into the waters (John 4:14).

But to what shall midday prayer be likened? Its refreshment for mind and spirit is like the bodily refreshment afforded by food and rest, as it is written, "They that wait upon the Lord shall renew their strength" (Isa. 40:31). Its cleansing of thoughts and of emotions is like the physical cleansing of a plunge in purifying waters, as it is written, "Wash me, and I shall be whiter than snow" (Ps. 51:7). Its clarifying of personal position and direction is like the orientation of a ship at sea by noontime sighting of the sun, as it is written, "In all thy ways acknowledge him, and he shall direct thy paths" (Prov. 3:6). Its quickening of our assurance that we are not alone is like the sudden touch upon our ear of a voice that is beloved, as it is written, "Be still, and know that I am God" (Ps. 46:10); and again, "I will never leave thee, nor forsake thee" (Heb. 13:5).

When, moreover, such prayer embodies intercession for fellow laborers whom one has lately seen and to whom one shortly must return, who shall set limits to its healing outreach or stay its flooding tide of power? For by the spiritual might which honest prayer releases, old hatreds and antagonisms may be overwhelmed, "immovable" prejudice may be swept aside, and the life of an enterprise or of a community may be lifted to new heights. Thus the incoming of the Spirit of Christ is like the incoming of the risen sea, which swallows up our man-made hindrances and sets new shore lines where it will, as it is written, "Old things are passed away; behold, all things are become new" (II Cor. 5:17).

How long for midday prayer? Perhaps five minutes—or more—or less.

We shall pray briefly before each meal.

Thus we acknowledge our creaturehood and our indebtedness to our Creator and Provider. It is good for a man, before he breaks bread, to recognize that by no ingenuity of his could he create so much as a single grain of wheat. To be sure, a man may cultivate and refine such wheat as he discovers on the earth; he may breed and crossbreed. Yet both the seed which the man manipulates and his own capacity for experiment and understanding are part of an amazing "givenness," with which the man himself has had nothing to do. "What hast thou," cries Paul, "that thou didst not receive?" (I Cor. 4:7.) And the psalmist likewise, "The earth is the Lord's, and the fulness thereof; the world, and they that dwell therein" (24:1).

It is therefore healthful for a man to empty himself of the pride of imagined independence, and to abase himself before his Maker, that he may be lifted up in humble confidence and established as a child of God (James 4:10). Indeed this act, which in Christian experience is at once repetitive and never ceasing; this act of taking God into our life by the humiliation of casting ourself upon him and unreservedly declaring our need; this very act is that which thrice each day we symbolize in the taking of bread into the body. Thus for the Christian every meal becomes a sacrament—which is to say, an outward and visible sign of an undeserved givenness that is inward and unseen. How indeed could such occasion be unaccompanied by thankful prayer?

So mealtime prayer, although its words be few, is charged with multiple meaning. By it we signify that we are creatures before the face of our Creator: wherefore we confess dependence utter and unconditional: "It is he that hath made us, and not we ourselves" (Ps. 100:3). Moreover, it is not in us to direct our own steps or to sustain our own life. Left to ourself we easily lose our way, and our soul quickly suffers leanness, and the face of the day and of our very thoughts becomes clouded with evil, and disaster, like a beast of prey, haunts our path: wherefore we commend ourself to God's protection and provision: for "we are his people, and the sheep of his pasture" (Ps. 100:3). Furthermore, because we have received incredible bounty, we praise our God with heart and voice: "Bless the Lord, O my soul, and forget not all his benefits" (Ps. 103:2).

Of all these things each piece of bread reminds us.

We shall pray on Sunday in public worship.

Why? For many reasons beyond the scope of this discussion, and for one reason which lies within it. This reason is that corporate prayer achieves a dimension unknown in private prayer.

But lest someone think that he has discovered the contrary when he has found only something else, let it be emphasized that we are discussing active prayer. This is different from congregational slumber or from a miscellany of individual dreams indulged in while the minister prays alone. Corporate prayer is different even from a profusion of private prayers simultaneously offered.

For corporate prayer, as the word itself tells us, is the united prayer of a body of praying people. It matters not whether the congregation pray in unison aloud or whether the words of the minister be its only utterance. What matters is that, through whichever voice, there be outpoured the common guilt, the common faith, the common care, the common praise, the common fervent supplication of the multitude. No minister alone can do this. No congregation, as individuals, can do it. But if the minister, acquainted in saving measure with the mind of Christ and with the needs of his people, strive Sunday after Sunday to do this with them, the congregation, praying as one man in its pastor's prayer, can do it through him. Thus prayer achieves new dimension, in which the prayer of the congregation becomes to the prayer of the individual as a surging wave of the ocean to a single drop of water.

When therefore with mind and heart we actively participate in public prayer, we are, in the familiar phrase, lifted out of ourself. We are enlarged in soul. Then when we return to individual life, something of that greater dimension lingers in us, so that our private prayer is vitalized and its horizons are expanded.

To what shall we liken this? Imperfectly we may compare it to a path which runs above the rocks beside the sea outside the window of the room where this is written. Throughout the year this path is trodden by men and women, many of whom are tired, many troubled. Here the solid rocks and the changing sky and the ever varied ocean present an aspect, now of power, now of peace, always of vastness and of never failing beauty.

Into those who love this walk some measure of these qualities appears to enter, so that the weary are refreshed, the weak are strengthened, the troubled find renewed perspective, and tasks of home and office are resumed as under an overarching loveliness. In this these men and women have gratefully responded to the impact of a physical dimension not to be met in home or street or office.

Similarly the vastness and the power and the peace of corporate prayer comprise dimensions of the spirit which we must go to corporate prayer to find. These in unique manner manifest the healing presence of Christ, who pronounced especial blessing upon united prayer: "Where two or three are gathered together in my name, there am I in the midst of them" (Matt. 18:20).

But if, as we have said, our private prayers are quickened through public worship, public worship is also made alert through private prayer. Thus the worship of a congregation accustomed throughout the week to pray in their own homes is astonishingly more alive than is the worship of an equal number of persons who try to pray only on some rare occasion when they are gathered together in the church.

We have called this difference astonishing. So indeed it is to experience. Yet perhaps it should not be so to thought. For surely those who daily rejoice, through private prayer, in the personal presence of Christ are they who should be most sensitive to his presence in public worship.

Is this the explanation of that difference? We know no other. But we know this: that during the days of Jesus' bodily presence there was in some groups to which he came an "electric" vitality, whereas in other groups there was a chilling deadness, with regard to which Matthew tells us that "he did not many mighty works there because of their unbelief" (13:58). Even so, corporate worship is more than an assemblage of men and women who coldly listen while another man speaks or prays. Corporate worship is united acceptance of God, for which private acceptance of God prepares us.

We know also another interesting thing. We know that in this alternation between corporate prayer and private prayer Jesus himself regularly took part. Luke tells us that "as his custom was, he went into the synagogue on the sabbath day" (4:16). Yet neither could the hunger of spirit of the congregation have been comparable to Jesus' yearning of soul; nor yet its diet, to the bread from heaven which was his daily sustenance (John 4:32). Again, in what things having to do with worship was not Jesus greater than those under whose leadership he joined in corporate prayer? More understandingly than they, he had gazed into the heart of man (John 2:25). More profoundly than they, he had fathomed the Scriptures (Mark 1:22). More intimately than they, he had walked with God (John 14:11). And he himself had prayed in such wise that heaven was torn open (Luke 3:21).

If ever man has had within him that which would

justify absence from public worship, Jesus would appear to be that man. Yet Jesus went "as his custom was," and engaged in corporate prayer. And as regards this act, by which the Lord of heaven and earth identified himself with unimpressive men and women, in common confession and common praise and common supplication, who shall say that blessing was not received by him, as well as given?

Even so great is the dimension of corporate prayer.

We shall pray unceasingly.

None but a fool, to be sure, or one deranged, would seek to carry on for so much as a single day an uninterrupted, audible monologue of prayer.

What then do we mean by unceasing prayer? We mean prayer in its most inclusive sense, as outlined in Chapter III. Perhaps before this present section is read, that chapter should again be scanned. For there we saw that prayer is more than spoken words: it is likewise those unuttered thoughts which are directed Godward. But prayer also is more than thought: it is a giving and receiving. And it is more, again, than an exchange of gifts: for prayer is the alerting of the ear of the soul. And it is more than listening: because, whether consciously or unawares, prayer is joining hands with God.

When therefore a man commits his life to God, he commits himself not to perpetual speech but to unceasing prayer—which is to say, to living in God's presence. So when Paul wrote to the Thessalonians, "Pray whithout ceasing" (I Thess. 5:17), he was not advocating an impossible exercise. Rather he was voicing sound wisdom: "Go with God into all that you do; and make the going and the deed, so far as in you lies, his choice." [2] To pray without ceasing, then, is so to relate ourself to God that all that we do is done for him, and in him, regardless of whether at any certain moment we happen to be thinking of God or not (Gal. 2:20; Phil. 1:20-21; I John 4:16).

To one who loves God this is seldom a burden. Instead it is pure joy. And when the burden must be taken up, as taken up it was upon the back of Jesus, in the form of a cross, then, if we remain faithful, the Presence and the Power, that is at once with us and within us, turns the burden into a radiance.

To what can unceasing prayer be likened? It is a bond between the soul and Christ like that between the ocean and the moon. Above the fundamental tide move major undulations of the spirit which culminate in corporate prayer. Riding on these are shorter waves which crest at stated intervals of private worship. Raised in turn upon the troughs and sides of these are countless little billows, brief ejaculations of praise, petition, intercession, which the quick breezes and currents of the day lift up. But undergirding all, persists the grand, inalienable bond, which moves us day after day, hour after hour, moment after moment, to reach toward him who is our light and strength.

Such are the inherent motions of prayer. We began this chapter by speaking of the seasons. We close it by mentioning the tides. Yet these may be two aspects of one truth. For prayer at its best is never a self-centered challenge to

---

[2] More will be said of this in Chapter VII, "Prayer in Varied Circumstance."

either the sunshine or the waters of God's mercy. And he who has learned to humble himself before the tides and seasons of the spirit, so as to throw in his strength with theirs, can pray, when trouble comes, with hope and confidence. For he will know of long experience that the Father's answer is better than the child's petition.

VI

How Shall We Pray?

✤✤✤✤✤✤✤✤✤✤✤✤✤✤✤✤✤✤✤✤✤✤✤✤✤✤✤✤✤✤✤✤✤✤

THERE ARE WAYS TO PRAY, AND THERE ARE WAYS NOT TO PRAY. The rules of prayer are simple. Yet we must abide them, lest our effort be in vain.

Some persons, for example, are helpless in the presence of a telephone. They have never learned the simple rules of its use. Yet how should they summon either fireman or friend by standing across the room and shouting demands toward an instrument whose receiver remained unlifted?

Other persons are helpless when confronted by the need to pray. Hence the question, How shall we do it?

We shall pray in the only way that a man can: by faith.

This is not to erect a barrier around prayer, shutting out the man who does not understand theology and is unwilling to array himself in a make-believe of doctrine. On the contrary, by proclaiming faith the condition of prayer the New Testament flings wide the door to every man who would come to God.

See what this faith is, and what it is not. The faith of which the New Testament sings is not a brocaded glove,

74

belying our earth-stained life, which we should unnaturally put on to shake hands with God. The Bible assures us that God, no less than any honorable man, despises all such falsification (Mark 12:40). What, then, is the faith that is required of prayer? The author of the Epistle to the Hebrews makes it very clear. He says, "He that cometh to God must believe that he is, and that he is a rewarder of them that diligently seek him" (11:6). In other words the faith without which a man cannot come to God is the unadorned disposition of his spirit that turns the man Godward. Who of us reaches to quench his thirst from a cup that he does not believe to be there, or that he believes to be empty? This very reaching for the cup is the faith that is required of prayer. It is as simple as that. What plain man in all the world would lift praying arms unless this faith leaped in his bosom: that God is, and that he is a rewarder of them that diligently seek him?

Such faith, to be sure, may move below the level of conscious thought, even in conflict with a doubting mind, so that a man may catch himself at prayer and say, "I don't believe in this!" But if he prays, he does believe, down where it counts. For the unconscious attitude is the one that determines life. The faith or unfaith that a man formulates has meaning only in so far as it expresses the hidden heart. Whatever, therefore, his protestations may be, that man who reaches out for God has in him the essential faith.

How gentle this requirement is! And how it puts to shame our complicated doubts and all pretended acts of worship, and, like an X ray, judges our inward parts! For if a man by the secret kneeling of his spirit may pray in the midst of his disbeliefs, he may, at another time, while thoughtlessly reciting words of prayer remain deeply estranged from God. Then those so-called prayers are not prayer, for they are not the action of faith; they are "vain repetitions" (Matt. 6:7), empty words, which body forth no outreach of the soul.

Jesus dwelt on it again and again, that always and only we come to God by faith. Not necessarily faith like a mountain that impresses us; far more often faith like a grain of mustard seed, so tiny a thing, so unspectacular, that it can cling to us while we are unaware of it, and pass unnoticed when we examine ourself to find it. Just enough faith to put forth the hand, even "on the chance," as it were—like that distraught father who appealed to Jesus, saying, "If thou canst do anything, have compassion on us, and help us" (Mark 9:22-24). The man's doubt, to be sure, had prompted that "if." But faith had cried, "Help us." And Jesus neither disregarded the doubt nor disappointed the faith. He dealt with the doubt by enlarging the faith that was in it; and he answered the faith by meeting the man's need. It is not important that we should never doubt; it is important that we exercise our faith by coming with our doubts to God.[1]

We shall pray honestly.

Some have been troubled, and have missed the true force of prayer, because they have thought that there were certain things that must be said when we pray. Then, although they could not sincerely say these things, they have reluctantly repeated them, because they have sincerely wished to pray. In such prayers, however, they have cor-

[1] Prayer in doubt and desolation will be discussed in Chapter VII.

rectly sensed a sound of hollowness. And sometimes they have mistakenly assumed that this falsity belonged to prayer itself. But no words ever are required in prayer which are discordant with our own condition as we ourself at that moment understand it before the face of God.

Let us never pretend to him who made us, and whose eyes are ever upon us, that we are other than we are. "God is not mocked," cries Paul (Gal. 6:7). And Jesus tells us in healing words of light, "God is a Spirit: and they that worship him must worship him in spirit and in truth" (John 4:24). This is part of what it means to come to God by faith: we must pray honestly.

When we pray, therefore, far from adopting any pious pose, we shall give up whatever mask of faith or of unbelief we may have previously put on, and we shall turn to the Almighty our natural face. We shall boldly declare our need and by no means conceal our doubt. We shall employ no language that we do not believe to be true. We shall ascribe to God nothing that we think is not his; we shall claim as our own nothing which our conscience tells us is not ours, whether sinfulness or goodness or aspiration or intention.

Later, of course, we may realize that more is ours, that more has long been ours, and that infinitely more belongs to God, than we can now believe. Then our prayers will grow accordingly. But today's prayer must represent us honestly today.

A certain man admired his neighbor's oak. So he bought a sapling and set it in the middle of his own lawn. But when he looked at it, it was such a slender thing that he was ashamed. He therefore went by night, and tore

77

branches from his neighbor's tree, and bound them to his sapling. But the little tree broke beneath their weight and all the branches died for lack of root. Then his neighbor came and reasoned with that man: "You fool!" he said. "You have trespassed on my land. You have spoiled my tree. You have ruined your own. You should have pruned that sapling until it was half the size it was, instead of trying to add to it. Then, if you had taken care of it, it would have spread out branches, and in time you could have sat in its shade. How do you think," he concluded, "that my tree began?"

To be sure, until one has done it and has seen the new uprush of strength, it takes courage to prune a scrawny little tree. For it seems that we shall cut away the life. Yet the life is not in that wood that we remove but in the root and column that we have thus set free to flourish.

Let us for this reason prune our prayers to the quick, however frail they now appear to be, until all that is left is bursting with life. Then let us faithfully nurture that life in God. Thus in course of time and in the fruitfulness of God's mercy our faith will increase and spread its branches, and in the heat of the day we shall have shade.

We shall pray intelligently.

Not all who have prayed have at all times and in all places of prayer prayed with the mind. Yet prayer that is unintelligent is ever in danger of becoming unworthy. Jesus spoke of loving the Lord our God with all our mind as well as with heart and soul and strength (Mark 12:30). And Paul admonished certain early Christians whose prayers were sometimes less than thoughtful, "I will pray with the spirit, and I will pray with the understanding also" (I Cor. 14:15) .

The Christian, then, is never content that prayer should remain merely "feeling," like that of the man who says, "I feel the presence of God, and this is enough." The Christian asserts that prayer is more than feeling, because we can pray regardless of feeling or absence of feeling, as Jesus prayed upon the cross, when, in the desolation of loneliness, he cried, "My God, my God, why hast thou forsaken me?" (Mark 15:34.)

There seems at first to be nothing in this prayer except that feeling of infinite aloneness. But when we look again we see that if nothing other than such feeling had been present, there could have been no prayer at all. For we do not pray when we are alone; we pray when we are with God. And Jesus, throughout his life, had not only felt the presence of God; he had understood God and had trusted God. Then, on the cross, understanding and faith conquered feeling, even while they gave it voice, as Jesus called upon him whom he knew to be never faraway, though in feeling he was as one abandoned.

Thus the understanding with which the Christian prays is like the understanding of friend by friend: it is the product not only of the mind's activity, which sometimes may be more active than mindful; it is the product of experience upon which reflection has worked. If, therefore, the friend whom we have come to understand be great in inward stature, our understanding of him may transform not only the demands we make upon his friendship but even our appraisal of our needs.

Why should it be otherwise with our friendship with

God? There was a foolish boy of whom Jesus spoke (Luke 15:11-24), who thought that he wanted his father's money. But when his father's cháracter dawned upon him he knew that most of all he needed that kind of friend. Then all that he asked for was forgiveness; and he received it and vastly more. But the father in the story is God, while that foolish youngster might be you or I. To be sure, we need food and clothing, as Jesus knew and underscored (Matt. 6:31-33). Yet sometimes, though we may not fully comprehend it, we stand in greater need of more-to-be than of more-to-wear.

The Christian therefore says that prayer, like all the rest of our experience, if it is to be intelligent, must be permitted to outdistance understanding. For example, whether we consciously pray or not, from moment to moment we live beyond our grasp. We fathom neither daily light nor love nor life. Yet we open our eyes; we build our homes; we eat and drink. If we should trim our earthbound venture to meet the measure of our understanding, how little we should do! Rather, our understanding grows by dealing understandingly with that which we have not yet understood.

Should we not do this also with prayer? Yet for every man who prays without thinking, there is another man who insists upon understanding before praying. Both of these men rob themselves. For if we should ask whether we trust God because we understand him or understand God because we trust him, the answer would be, "Both." For faith and understanding, where they are engaged together, interact upon each other and help each other, like two climbers in a difficult place.

We shall, if we be wise, pray persistently.

This persistence of Christian prayer is not, though to a passer-by it might appear to be, like that of a shipwrecked mariner, day after day waving his shirt and screaming to attract attention. For we are already in God's attention far more than God is in our attention. This good news the Old Testament declares again and again, and the New Testament is rapturous with it from cover to cover. When we truly pray, therefore, we commune with a God who has sought and found us, whose ear is bent low, like the ear of a father above his child.

Nor is persistence in prayer necessary in order to break down unwillingness on the part of God to give us good things. When Jesus told those stories of the man who wakened his neighbor at midnight to borrow bread for an unexpected guest (Luke 11:5-8), and of the poor widow who plagued an unjust judge until he granted justice (Luke 18:2-5), the fact was underscored that both of these petitioners were successful only because of what we today would call their "nuisance value." So much is clear to everyone who reads. What is less generally realized is that Jesus never says of these stories, "Prayer is like that." Rather, he bids us be of good courage because prayer is not like that. His argument is: if persistent petition wins assent from an evil and reluctant man, how much more shall our prayers be granted by a holy and loving heavenly Father who is infinitely more eager to give us good things than a human parent to give food to his child (Luke 11:11-13; Matt. 7:9-11).

Whether we shall receive, therefore (not necessarily

that seeming good which we desire, but that best thing which God is waiting to bestow), depends not upon God's unconcern to give but upon our slowness to ask: for "Every one that asketh receiveth" (Luke 11:10). And any uncertainty as to whether we shall find treasure in God, is not because the treasure may not be there, but because we may be too indifferent to seek it: Jesus assures us, and our own experience testifies, that "he that seeketh findeth" (Luke 11:10). And if the door of the kingdom of heaven appears to be shut against us, we need but come with Jesus' invitation in our hands and knock, and "to him that knocketh it shall be opened" (Luke 11:10).

Yet in our asking and seeking and knocking there is need of persistence. What man can bestow his best friendship upon a neighbor who raps at his door but once? Or what father, though his resource be more than enough, can provide education for a son who only momentarily seeks it? This boy besought his father to educate him, before he knew how hard it would be to keep on asking in the only way that would make him a learned man. The father was able, and yearned to help him. The son was gifted of mind. Yet he left school to make merry with his friends, and his unusual capacities and opportunities remained unexplored. To be sure, this boy once asked for that which is high, but soon he wearied of asking; he sought, but the treasure that he found was not easy to dig; he knocked, and the door was opened, but then he went out and did not return.

To put it differently: what man ever built a house with one blow of the hammer?

We shall pray humbly.

But what does this mean? It does not mean whining, like neglected offspring to a neglectful mother. Nor yet does it mean groveling, like a slave before a brutal master. The Christian when he prays neither cringes nor whimpers. He comes to God with that same exalted lowliness with which a loving and trustful child climbs to the lap of an understanding parent. Perhaps this was in Jesus' thought when he spoke of receiving the kingdom of God as a little child or else being unable to enter it at all (Mark 10:15).

We shall pray, therefore, as confiding children to a listening Father, full of our child-needs and child-desires, telling him all our hopes and fears, and resting the issue in his love. And when his embrace has made us bold, we shall declare outright the treasure on which our heart is set, and then we shall leave the issue with his love. We shall remember that children have tried to run from that which earthly parents have known to be their safeguard, as for example the sharp thrust of inoculation. We shall remember, too, that children have pleaded for that which would destroy them—a stick of dynamite, or a ball of candy held in the hand of a tubercular peddler. So, although we tell our Father all things, we shall trust the issue to his love.

We shall pray in acceptance of our Father's gifts, both of the past and of today. If there be blessings which he has meant for us that we have left scattered about unopened —how many there probably are!—we shall at once begin to investigate them and to praise him anew. The New Testament is given us: why not feed upon it and make it our own? Prayer is given us: why not explore it? Light is given us: why not walk in it and forsake those deceptive shadows? Forgiveness is offered us: why not take up our abode in that, until it is that from which we depart and to which we return, like a bird to her nest? If we should daily name to God a mere half-dozen blessings which come to mind in prayer, accept them for our own, and make them part of life, our whole outlook and being could be renewed.[2]

We shall pray in realization that God deals with us as with sons, and that "whom the Lord loveth he chasteneth" (Heb. 12:6). We shall seek throughout all discipline to learn of him, to grow in understanding, and to increase in the power of his Spirit; knowing this, that because his disciplines are of love, the communion of child-mind with Father-mind need never be broken, even in pain, even in grief, and that he himself is our inestimable reward.

We shall pray as created ones to our Creator; for we were made by him, not he by us. His, not ours, is the power. His, not ours, is the wisdom. So why should we dictate policy? The will that must be done is not our own but his. We shall therefore diligently seek his will, that we may do it; and when it is clear, we shall not negatively, but affirmatively, receive it. For our positive will, our passionate will, is that his will be done; and if at any time our will be otherwise, then we shall pray that in God's mercy our wayward purpose may be changed, until it serves as eager instrument of his.

We shall tell all things to our Father, and be silent. And ever and again he will speak.

[2] But it is futile to try to count blessings which we cannot see as blessings. This was discussed in Chapter IV.

We shall pray in the name of Jesus.

But lest anyone suppose that this is magic, let us at once make clear that this is so far magic's opposite that it is part of what we mean by praying intelligently. For whereas magic makes no demand, in respect of spirit or understanding or intent, of him who uses it, prayer in the name of Jesus searches with a light more bright than daylight and tests with fire that is more revealing than that of a refiner's crucible the spirit and understanding and intent of him who prays.

Suppose, for example, that a man should fall upon profane knees and beg his heavenly Father that cancer might overtake his rival. Suppose, moreover, that the man should try to seal his plea and to guarantee its result by closing his prayer with the words "in Jesus' name." Two fallacies would straightway be apparent. First, the man would have sought to use the phrase "in Jesus' name" as a magic wand. Secondly, the man would not have prayed in Jesus' name: he would have prayed only in the name of his own degraded desire.

But the words "in the name of Jesus Christ our Lord" express the very mood and purpose of the prayer that is truly offered in his name; they tell us of the daily hunger and the daily bread of him who rightly utters them; they intimate at least the hope, and often the reality, of a personal relationship with Christ in which prayer is essential for that relationship's development; they show the Spirit of Jesus moving in a praying man and reaching through that man into the world about him.

To pray, then, in Jesus' name is to let our prayer become a highway for Christ's Spirit. This requires that we seek to understand him as he is found in the New Testament and in our own heart and in our fellow men. To pray in Jesus' name is to turn our personal encounter with Christ into thankful obedience to him, so that increasingly he becomes a controlling force in daily life. In so far, therefore, as prayer is the breathing of a living soul, prayer in Jesus' name is the inhalation and exhalation of the Spirit of Christ.

How personal, yet how broadly human, the need of this is! For of what value is the life of the world, the life that consists in possessions and activities and institutions, except as there be inward life, the life of the soul, to give it meaning and support? Today, as everyone will tell us, inventiveness has so outdistanced morality that our cleverness threatens us with extinction. It may be less commonly recognized that morality falters because the soul that breathes only dust is stifled. Hence few are good enough or wise enough or strong enough to manage our world well, or even their own house: count the delinquent children; count the divorces.

What, then, is our most urgent want, if not a saving measure of the goodness and wisdom and power of God? But how shall these become ours? They are found, the New Testament joyfully declares, in Christ, in whom God himself took flesh and dwelt among us (I Cor. 1:24, 30). The goodness and wisdom and power of God accordingly become ours as we participate in honest prayer in Jesus' name. Such prayer embraces all compassion, all forgiveness, all enlightenment, all healing, as well as incidentals like necessary food and clothing. And the community of the praying is the kingdom of God.

Prayer in the name of Jesus is a conduit carrying to the desert of our weakness and wickedness and folly the reclaiming waters of God's purity and wisdom and strength. Prayer in Jesus' name is the arm of the soul which we extend to bless beyond our physical ability. "Hitherto," said Jesus, "ye have asked nothing in my name: ask, and ye shall receive, that your joy may be full" (John 16:24).

VII

Prayer In Varied Circumstance

✤✤✤✤✤✤✤✤✤✤✤✤✤✤✤✤✤✤✤✤✤✤✤✤✤✤✤✤✤

LET US NOW EXAMINE PRAYER AS IT APPEARS IN VARIED CIR-
cumstance. Here we shall look particularly not for those
aspects of prayer which are common to changing situations
but rather for the peculiarity of each condition with reference to prayer.

We shall pray in the midst of doubt and desolation.

Probably every man who has ever tried to walk with God
has at one time, or at many times, stumbled, seemingly
alone, beneath a sky of brass. Indeed, many such experi-
ences have been recorded, even in the Bible. For example,
from the mouth of Job,[1] one of the Old Testament's he-
roic men of God, pours the following lament: "Oh that I
knew where I might find him. . . . Behold, I go forward,
but he is not there; and backward, but I cannot perceive
him: on the left hand, where he doth work, but I cannot
behold him: he hideth himself on the right hand, that I
cannot see him" (23:3, 8-9).

Another man reports his search for God in words no

[1] We are told that the book of Job is a drama. But what biography has
been more compact of the very stuff of life?

88

less discouraging: "Clouds and thick darkness are round about him" (Ps. 97:2 R.S.V.). Yet the psalmists, of whom this man was one, were they who wrote those beautiful outpourings of the soul which, more than any other single group of writings, have enriched the hymnbooks and prayer books of the Church. So this man's doubt and desolation were not the final facts. For, as we shall later see, in the midst of these discouragements he gave himself to that which leads beyond them.

Even in the brighter light of the New Testament we find the Son of God himself sharing our bitter question, "My God, my God, why hast thou forsaken me?" (Mark 15:34.) Yet here again, doubt and desolation were not conclusive.

Now: for one content to remain in the solitary confinement of hopelessness, such "disillusionment" as that of Job or of the psalmist or of Jesus might easily constitute the final bolting of the door against the mercies of heaven. Then we might state our case like this: "We have sought the face of God, but we have been shut in darkness. We have served God, but in our deepest need he has left us helpless. What kind of God is that!" And the empty sky would seem to answer, "There is no God at all."

But the prison of doubt is unlike many prisons, for in this prison the lock is on the inside. Hence the first act of any man who would be delivered from the darkness of his disbelief is to draw that bolt, that Christ may come to him within the prison, prior to leading him out of the prison into the day, as it is written, "Behold, I stand at the door, and knock: if any man hear my voice, and open the door, I will come in to him, and will sup with him, and he with me" (Rev. 3:20).

What then is this act which unbolts the door? It is an act of prayer—which is to say, it is an act of our whole being, wherewith, walled round by doubts, we affirm the faith that looks upon these doubts and knows them to be faithless; and, besieged by shadows, we acclaim those glimmers of the light which fissures in our doubts let through.

It is like a man who built himself a cabin with shelves around the walls. One evening this man was visited by a friend who was a carpenter. As the evening progressed, the carpenter became noticeably restless. When the host inquired as to the cause of that uneasiness, the carpenter replied, "If you'll forgive me, it's those shelves. Every one of them slopes down toward the right."

"Do they?" exclaimed the owner of the cabin. "I never noticed."

But why was the carpenter disturbed, whereas the other man was not? The carpenter was troubled because he saw those shelves against a true vertical, which ran like a plumb line through his mind. The owner of the cabin, on the other hand, was at ease with crookedness, and even unaware of it, because no perpendicular penetrated his thought. And the carpenter, if ever that plumb line should leave his consciousness, would neither see any more that things were sloping nor know the hour of his abandonment.

Thus we sense our desolation because we know a Presence. Desolation, therefore, is not extinction of communion, as it appears to be; but it is grievous reduction of it. The communion remaining within the limitation is that which makes the limitation painful. For if God should utterly forsake a man, that man would be so dead that he would breathe no syllable of forsakenness.

It is likewise with doubt: our doubts trouble us only as we view them against the true vertical of faith. Which is to say, unless we be possessed of more than doubts, we do not complain of doubts. Which is to say, again, no man bewails darkness unless he believes in light.

So when a young man came to an old minister, and sat down in the minister's study, and blurted, "I don't believe in God!" the old man kindly replied, "Nevertheless, that is not why you are here."

But the young man, feeling that this was no time for fooling, inquired, with a certain sharpness in his voice, as to what the minister meant.

"I mean," said the old man, "that it is not doubt which wearies of doubting; it is faith. Doubt is lifeless and unfeeling, like the husk about a grain of wheat. But faith is the living germ itself, which presses against the confinement of disbelief, and suffers, and complains. If you were full of nothing but the dead chaff of doubt, you would be untroubled.

"Therefore," the old man continued, "when you came to me to say that you did not believe in God, your very confession of doubt was an utterance of faith. And it was faith which brought you here, not doubt. Let us now get at that faith, and see what we can do about it."

Then the young man was amazed as the faith within him was uncovered. For he found that he could truly pray a very simple prayer. So he drew the bolt of his prison

91

house, and invited Christ to come in; and the invitation was not ignored.

This is what Job did in his desolation. Listen: "I cannot see [God]," he cried: "But he knoweth the way that I take: when he hath tried me, I shall come forth as gold" (23:9-10). In other words, like the servant in one of Jesus' parables, Job gave himself in loyal obedience to an absent Master (Matt. 24:45-46), because he longed to be found worthy upon his Master's return. And the Master did return, and Job rejoiced with joy that was greater than before, saying:

> I had heard of thee by the hearing of the ear;
> But now mine eye seeth thee.
>
> —42:5 A.S.V.

Thus prayerful, faithful commitment to One whose nearness he could nowise sense was the unlocking of Job's desolation.

In like manner the psalmist no sooner had remarked upon the clouds and darkness which surround the Lord, than he turned his gaze from that bewilderment and found the solid rock on which a man might dare to climb even into the heart of mystery,

Clouds and thick darkness are round about him;
   righteousness and justice are the foundation of his throne.
                                        —97:2 R.S.V.

There, in the midst of doubt, is faith that it is better to be righteous than unrighteous, better to be just than unjust; faith, moreover, that this is so because God himself is just and righteous. Let any man prayerfully spend his life in behalf of that belief, and one day he will lift his eyes to behold no more clouds but the unveiled face of him whom he has served by faith.

It was not otherwise upon the cross, with Jesus. For when in his forsakenness he cried, "My God, my God, why . . . ?" (Mark 15:34.) the very words of doubt, as we have earlier seen,[2] were prayer; and the protest of desertion was itself communion. Then throughout seeming desolation he did for God the only thing he still could do: he continued to abide in faithfulness and love. And we who look upon that cross declare that God worked mightily within that faithfulness and that God was that very love. So the bolt was drawn; the door was opened; the Presence was revealed. And Jesus' final words were words of confidence and of realized fellowship: "Father, into thy hands I commend my spirit" (Luke 23:46) .

Always there persists within our desolation an uncomprehended comradeship and care. This may be likened to that between a child and a loving parent while the child sleeps. For the parent comes, and gently touches the child, and finds that he is cold, and lifts another blanket over him, and steals away, out of the child's sight though the child should open his eyes, but never beyond concern. And the child, through the semiconsciousness of sleep, may feel the parent bending over him and the cover laid in place, so that he is stirred with gratitude. Or he may remain in the aloneness of insensibility until the morning, and only then discover that in his helplessness love had drawn near and had ministered to him. Thus indeed a

[2] Chapter VI

heavy mist of incomprehension, like the thick cloud of sleep, sometimes envelopes us. Then, although God visits us with merciful provision, and himself stands beside us, we may remain unknowing until the numbness passes from our soul. Yet throughout all it is only we who are unconscious of God; God is never unconscious of us.

Meanwhile there is much that we can do. If, for example, the fog in which we are wrapped has been of our own thoughtless or determined making, we may at once begin to unmake it, like that small boy playing with his friends at the end of the block. Suddenly, in the midst of play, the boy felt hungry. Then he began to listen. Then through the babel of his friends' voices he heard his mother calling him. "Why didn't you come before?" she asked as he climbed the steps. "I've been calling you for a quarter of an hour!"

"Oh," he replied, "the fellows were yelling around. I didn't hear you." Which was true. Yet he heard when he wanted to hear.

Therefore if a man has immersed himself in the clamor of the world or has encased his heart in a callus of misdeeds, the remedy for that man's isolation from Home should be simple and clear. For that man is called throughout more than a quarter of an hour. He is not only called; he is sought. He is not only sought; he is besieged with mercies. And the remedy for that man's desolation may be as simple as opening his ears and his eyes and his heart; as simple as turning and consenting to be found. But this alerting of the soul, this turning of the soul, this consent of the soul, is prayer.

Moreover, although the curtain of separation between

ourself and God be not constituted of our willful act, it is nevertheless an earth-bound thing, and not a heavenly. The clouds, for example, that obscure the sun are never around the sun but only around the earth. They are, in fact, the reaction of our earth's atmosphere to the rays of that effulgence which they hide. Likewise from hardship, or from ill health, or from physical pain, or from grief, may rise an isolating overcast which may fill our thought with questioning.

In such condition it is a help to realize that the opposite of doubt is never knowledge. This helps because our very natural cry for knowledge must be futile so long as we remain in doubt and desolation; and for full knowledge, so long as we inhabit a mortal body (I Cor. 13:12). Which is to say, our condition is itself a barrier, perhaps the greatest barrier, to understanding our condition. So we praise God that the opposite of doubt is not knowledge but faith; and that the opposite of desolation is not knowledge but enlarged communion. For so, in the midst of loneliness and contradiction, by remaining faithful in life and in prayer, faith and communion may be nurtured, until they issue in understanding.

For we do not know in order that we may believe; we believe in order that we may know. Hence faith, whether accompanied by knowledge or temporarily without knowledge, is beyond price. For of it are the springs both of knowledge and of life. But knowledge without faith is darker than ignorance.

How many times a parent is able to say no more than this! For how should a three-year-old know his parent's purpose or his parent's love or his parent's sacrifice in permitting the doctor, for example, to break a crooked leg, in order that it may be straightened? What can the parent say, except, "Trust me, dear one; and someday you may know?"

Then if the child refuses to trust, preferring to believe his doubts than to believe his parent; and if he rejects the comfort and enrichment of limited communion with his parent, because the carefree communion of happiness has been withdrawn; and if he cries, "No! No! if you loved me, you wouldn't let this happen!" and if he fans within his heart the fires of bitterness and rebellion—if the child does this, he renders impotent his parent's eagerness to console him, and he inflicts upon himself how great loss.

So Jesus grieved because the people of a certain city, by rejecting him instead of trusting him, made it impossible to bless them. Yet this divine frustration is not of one occasion only but of all the years, because of all God's little ones who turn against him, believing him to have neglected them. Listen; for in these words groans the desert wind of every desolation: "How often would I have gathered thy children together, as a hen doth gather her brood under her wings, and ye would not! Behold, your house is left unto you desolate" (Luke 13:34-35).

So we thank God that the saving word is not knowledge. For knowledge, especially in certain circumstance, may lie beyond our reach. And though it lay within our grasp, it would still be dust and ashes, without faith. But prayer can stir in any heart, and fall from any lips, at any time. Even in the midst of desolation prayer can quicken communion; and in the midst of doubt, likewise, prayer can establish faith. And faith, in time, can lead us into such understanding as we are able to entertain.

The key is prayer. It is like a small child who awoke in darkness in a house of silence. There could, he knew, be none besides himself in a house so quiet and so dark. Finding himself in desolation, the child became rigid with fear, so as to be almost voiceless. Yet he managed a kind of croaking cry for his absent parent. Then to his amazed delight his parent answered from another bed in the same room.

But God is always in the same room. When we call upon him, he never fails us.

We shall pray in time of sorrow.

To be sure, grief, and the physical exhaustion which accompanies it, may cast us, as it were, into a dungeon of separation from heaven, and there let loose upon us a stinging swarm of doubts. Such doubt and desolation have been the subject of the last few pages.

Or grief may bring upon us an almost overwhelming human loneliness. But we shall later consider loneliness under its own name. Here we write of sorrow itself.

Grief, nevertheless, holds this in common with other of life's crises, that, when it falls upon a man, he is advantaged if he has some knowledge of prayer. Then, as one shipwrecked might say to himself, "At least I know how to row a boat," so this man might say, "At least I know how to pray."

Assuredly, a man unacquainted with prayer may learn, even in sorrow, to pray; though to begin to do so at such a time may be nearly as difficult as first to take hold of the

97

oars of a boat in a storm at sea. There are those who prefer to sink: of their own will they submit to being swallowed by grief, so that they never rise again. Of all such, Rachel is the mother, Rachel vividly pictured "weeping for her children, and would not be comforted, because they were not" (Matt. 2:18). Yet if they "were," she would need no comfort. So, because she needs comfort, she rejects comfort, and sets her will to sink rather than to row, to be destroyed by darkness rather than to pray her way into the light. Even Almighty God, as we have earlier observed, is frustrated by a human will which perversely clings to misery and turns away from consolation.

But we may learn to pray in sorrow. We may begin by praying for a determined will to co-operate with God in such wise as to conquer sorrow. This prayer, to be sure, may be halfhearted. Nevertheless let us not fail to offer it. For half a heart or half a prayer is better than no heart or no prayer, because in prayer, as in all things else, we arrive at the greatest by beginning with the least. So if we ask today with little more than our lips for the will to co-operate wholeheartedly with God, tomorrow we may ask with all that is in us, and receive his comfort in our whole being.

It is like the building of a bridge. Those weighty cables no man could fling across that river. Yet a kite may carry over a thread; and the thread may drag a string across; and the string may pull a rope from shore to shore; and the rope may tow a cable; and the cable, a cable of cables. Now the bridge supports metropolitan traffic. But when first we saw it, it was a solitary cable which, still earlier, had been a single thread.

Thus the bridge between heaven and earth, which is prayer, before it carries unceasing traffic of the angels of God, ascending and descending (Gen. 28:12), begins as a very slender thing, no more impressive than a thread. In sorrow this first fragile filament of prayer is flung to us from God, that we may welcome it with eager heart and draw down blessings after it. But what is this, so rich with hope, so easily broken? It is our least desire to co-operate with God in the conquest of our grief. So we grasp it with prayer.

Then as determination to work this out with God becomes more strong in us, we pray to be delivered from self-pity, and from bitterness, and from such concern with our own imperfect wishes as would insulate us from the perfect wish of God in our behalf. We pray, accordingly, that God will open our eyes and hearts to all of those unimagined blessings which this experience especially fits us to recognize and to accept.

Perhaps by now we shall be strengthened to offer a petition yet more difficult, for we are striving more and more to find God's perfect wish for us within our broken circumstance, knowing that God's perfect wish is perfect blessing. So if we are able, we now pray that with heart and soul and mind we may accept, as the basis of God's continuing compassions, the condition which has caused our sorrow. But if our spirit fails us, then we shall pray persistently for God's enablement, that we may be made equal even to this. For only after we have acknowledged the position in which we find ourself, shall we be able to receive those consolations and enrichments with which, in infinite mercy, our position is surrounded.

It is like a man who owned a business with branches in many lands. This man called his son and said to him, "I have put you in charge of the office in such-and-such a country. It will be a broadening experience for you. You will learn much there that you could not learn elsewhere. And I have many friends in that place whom you will be enriched by knowing. The door to every good thing will be opened to you. I have seen to that. Go in high confidence, for you will be made more than welcome."

Then the young man was filled with sorrow, for he was content to stay where he was. He had no desire to be broadened or to be inwardly enriched. And he shrank from wrestling with unfamiliar responsibility.

Yet he went, because his father required it. And having arrived in that country, he began to become acquainted. But because he loved ease and hated toil, he welcomed invitations to dinner and he avoided going to his office. So the business declined, and the young man fell into disrepute, and he never acquired those good things which his father had made possible for him, and even his father's long-time friends ceased to invite him to their homes.

Then with heaviness of heart the old man recalled his son. He said to him, "My son, unusual opportunities have been yours. But you have disdained them. Therefore, until you have shown a change of mind, I cannot give you the wealth which I have kept for you. Go now, and clear the boulders from such-and-such a field of mine."

So the young man went out, reviling his father and cursing his luck.

Which is to say once more, when God places us in charge of a sorrow, he seeks to make our new position advantageous with manifold good things. But in order to take these good things into our heart, we must embrace the assignment upon which they are conditioned. An example of this is in the Gospels, for Jesus became our supreme light only after he had turned full-face toward the cross. Then more than the cross was given him; for the whole support and sustenance of God were his in that obedience. This is memorialized in the account of the Transfiguration (Mark 9:2). Paul also dwells upon it with unavoidable implication that the name which is above every name would not be Christ's if he had died upon the cross without inwardly accepting the cross (Phil. 2:8-9). Even so, whenever with our own prayer we ratify the difficult appointment to preside over a sorrow, doors of promise open to us on the right hand and on the left.

One of these is the door of human sympathy, which, as the word itself tells us, means "suffering with" another. But to sorrow with another is to enter upon deeper and truer friendship. It is also in profound sense to become human. For once we advance beyond the merely physical, sorrow is probably the largest common denominator of mankind. Wherefore he who has never known affliction has yet to become wholly a man, and he who has shared only his neighbor's pleasure has still to become a friend. Where else indeed is to be found such depth of comradeship as that of sorrow with sorrow? Hence earth's most compelling friendship is with that Man who, more than other men, was "a man of sorrows, and acquainted with grief" (Isa. 53:3).

Thus a second door is opened, the door of larger understanding of Jesus. For, press as far as we can go in sorrow, we are still outdistanced by the Son of Man, while every separate grief of ours becomes interpreter of some greater grief of his. So by our sorrow the Scriptures are unclosed as a newfound Book and the Christian life is revealed to us as a life hitherto almost unknown. Therefore we kneel in thankfulness to him who, through the twin doors of sympathy, has disclosed to us a new humanity and a new Christ.

But more: as we become identified with Christ in grief, he becomes identified with us in power, until the light that was his becomes our light; and his secret joy sings at the heart of our own sorrow; and, as with angel's wings, the weight is lifted which otherwise would crush us.

Yet more: as through the door of sympathy with Christ power from on high flows into us, so, through the door of sympathy with sorrowing mankind this selfsame power flows out from us in healing (John 7:37-38). Hear Paul as he exults in this receiving and outgiving of God's mercy: "Blessed be the God and Father of our Lord Jesus Christ, the Father of mercies and God of all comfort, who comforts us in all our affliction, so that we may be able to comfort those who are in any affliction, with the comfort with which we ourselves are comforted by God" (II Cor. 1:3-4 R.S.V.).

Such thankful prayer as this, implemented by kindly deed and strengthening word, may well be ours. What incredible power this is, and with what glad faithfulness we should both welcome and employ it, this power that is given us through sorrow! So the best thing that a sorrowing person can do is to pray. And next best thing is to arise from his knees and go to the home of his sorrowing neighbor and bring him such cheer as he can.

But how shall we visit sorrow? We must not wait until we feel able. For then we should never go. For whatever any man can bring to his sorrowing friend must appear in his own eyes utterly trivial as against the sorrow itself. Yet in the providence of God, when a man sorrows, his friend's least kindness is rendered great. Even so, if we be at all sensitive, we shall never visit sorrow except as Paul visited the Corinthians, "in weakness, and in fear, and in much trembling" (I Cor. 2:3).

On the way to our neighbor's house we shall pray that Christ, who will be there with him, will administer our gift as he administered those few loaves upon the hillside, which in themselves were so ridiculously small before the hunger of the multitude (Mark 6:34-44). We shall commit to him our good intention, and the compassion that we feel but do not know how to show, and our remembrance of our own sorrow which has quickened our understanding, and our recollection of the comfort which has strengthened us, and our present offering of word or of wordless deed, and we shall pray that he will do with these as he did with the loaves.

So prayer in sorrow can fill us with joy. Prayer in darkness can surround and penetrate us with light. And this light is stronger than darkness, and this joy is deeper than grief. Moreover, in our sorrowing world our prayer can turn our sorrow into the merciful instrument of God's outreaching love.

We shall pray in suffering and sickness.

We shall, of course, also resort to the best physician available. Yet, side by side with healing of the body, we shall seek healing of the spirit. For to care only for that which is without, and to neglect that which is within, would be as though a man should prize his dwelling more highly than his life.

For example, there was a man who lived alone in a little house. When a hurricane came and blew down his house, and a falling beam crushed the man's arm, are we to suppose that the man called only for carpenters to rebuild his home, and not for a physician to cleanse his wound and save his life? Yet as a man's house is to his body, so is a man's body to his soul.

In suffering and sickness, then, we shall pray, in order that the deep places of our being may be made whole. Indeed flesh and spirit are so mysteriously intertwined that the restoring of the soul may powerfully affect the healing of the body. It is as though the man just mentioned, with his wound cleansed and his shattered arm beginning to knit, should go by night, after the carpenters had left his house, and, with his free hand, further the work that they had done by day, so that in the morning, when the carpenters returned and saw what had been done, they would stand amazed.

Contrariwise, a spirit injured and unhealed may strive in secret to defeat the body's cure; as though our man, with wound inflamed and with infected mind, should steal through darkness with an ax and mutilate the work which he himself had asked the carpenters to do.

So when a certain man was brought to Jesus with palsy

of the body, Jesus, looking upon him with seeing eyes, healed first the palsy of his soul, and said to him, "Son, thy sins be forgiven thee" (Mark 2:5) . It was only after this that Jesus said to him, "Arise, . . . and go thy way" (Mark 2:11) . Likewise the psalmist in one breath praises God, not for one reviving benefit, but for two: "Bless the Lord, O my soul . . . : who forgiveth all thine iniquities; who healeth all thy diseases" (103:2-3) .

In suffering and sickness, therefore, while each day we open heart and mind to receive and to absorb into our life God's perfect will, we rightly pray for strengthening both of spirit and of body. Yet this perfect will of God, in which, as earlier observed, lies our true blessing—this perfect will of God, not despite its perfectness, but because of it, may so exceed our dust-clouded imagination that we may fail to see that it is acceptable at all, just as a small child may fail to appreciate disciplinary action which is designed for his well-being in later years.

More than one sufferer, supposing that whatever contradicted his own idea of the good and the plausible must be either impossible or evil, has striven against the will of God and lost its benediction. Yet not only evil threatens the good; the better and the best also eagerly displace it. So in suffering and sickness we wisely pray that we may never cling to our imagined good in such wise as to turn away God's unimaginable best. "For my thoughts are not your thoughts, neither are your ways my ways, saith the Lord. For as the heavens are higher than the earth, so are my ways higher than your ways, and my thoughts than your thoughts." (Isa. 55:8-9.)

God's perfect will, God's unimaginable best, may mean

the healing of our flesh when earth's authoritative wisdom shakes its head and counts the hours left to us.

Again, God's perfect will, God's matchless blessing, may mean a spirit purified and strengthened by the strength and purity of Christ (I John 3:3), reigning within a broken body, whose very brokenness affirms the wonder of that power (II Cor. 4:7).

Listen to one who learned this lesson out of anguish, as every man must learn it who does learn it. Hear Paul as he describes the lesson of suffering in his own flesh: "For this thing I besought the Lord thrice, that it might depart from me. And he said unto me, My grace is sufficient for thee: for my strength is made perfect in weakness. Most gladly therefore will I rather glory in my infirmities, that the power of Christ may rest upon me" (II Cor. 12:8-9).

Clearly this is far from negative resignation. This is passionate acquisition (Phil. 3:8), as though the man in our earlier story, when his little house blew down, should find that its hollow walls were packed with gold, making him rich above the rich men of his city. How much negative resignation would then exist in that man's heart? Would he not exult with joy? Yet the fulfillment in our life of God's perfect will is more rewarding than gold. And God's will may be furthered, both in ourself and in the world, through prayer in sickness and suffering.

Men before now have locked themselves in cells, that they might devote a lifetime to intercession for the world. But if a man who thinks himself useless, because he is locked in an incurable body, should spend his remaining life in intercession for his fellow men, what inestimable blessing might flow forth from that man's prisoned hope!

Thus suffering and sickness are redeemed from waste, and turned into profit. For, as in sorrow, if we seek to advance the will of God, and not alone our own immediate desire, here may be vigorous upgrowing of the soul. Here may be quickening of perception. Here may be strengthening of sympathy. Here may be usefulness undreamed of. Here in our own flesh may be enthroned the very power that worked in Jesus, who shared upon the cross the body's ultimate pain and made of it, in the light of Easter, our ultimate encouragement.

We shall pray in wakefulness.

For here is time, if we have had difficulty finding time, to pray. Here while we lie awake is uninterpreted leisure. So we turn wakefulness into worship, fretfulness into adoration, and tossing upon our bed into repose upon "the everlasting arms" (Deut. 33:27).

To be sure, sleep is needful for the body. In this our heavenly Father, who loves us better than we love ourself, is not unconcerned. Yet the essence of sleep is restoration, and this, in amazing measure, may be ours through prayerful quietness. Then when drowsiness comes upon us, it finds us with our taut strings loosed, our knots untied, our sins forgiven, and our whole being ready to receive the benefit of sleep.

How then shall we pray in wakefulness? Perhaps in part after the manner suggested in Chapter V for evening prayer. But here is opportunity for wide-reaching intercession and thanksgiving, for leisurely thinking about God, and for enjoyment of his presence.

Accordingly we let our thought range across the needs

of relatives and loved ones, of friends and casual acquaintances and those whom we dislike, of men who carry heavy burdens of responsibility, of sufferers and those who, like us, lie awake. As we remember each of these, we pray in his behalf.

We recall also the multitude of God's blessings. We try to name them. We thank him for each one.

We think of God himself as he has come to us in Christ, and in this thinking we commune with him, until our wakeful prayer is like the converse of friend with friend (John 14:15-18). Thus the psalmist, though he had never looked upon the face of Christ, was still, because of what he knew of God, filled with joy while he lay awake. "My soul," he cried, "shall be satisfied as with marrow and fatness; and my mouth shall praise thee with joyful lips: when I remember thee upon my bed, and meditate on thee in the night watches" (63:5-6).

It is fitting also that we pray for sleep, and that we then accept with thankful hearts the rest which God bestows.

We shall pray in human loneliness.

For to him who remains faithful in prayer God remains faithful in comradeship which no forsakenness of earth can shatter. Such was the experience of Paul, who wrote to his young friend Timothy, "All men forsook me. . . . Notwithstanding the Lord stood with me, and strengthened me" (II Tim. 4:16-17). Such is the assurance of Jesus to those who would follow him, "If a man love me, he will keep my words: and my Father will love him, and we will come unto him, and make our abode with him" (John 14:23).

This is the comradeship which is the secret wealth within all other wealth. Lacking this, the millionaire is but a shoeless beggar. This is the comradeship devoid of which the fellowship of men is as a wind-blown desert. This is the comradeship which makes a garden of a wilderness and, as the psalmist tells us, turns a vale of tears into a place of springs (84:5-6). This comradeship alone might be worth all else that a man has, if such were the price of it.

But with this comradeship is given another. It is the joyful kinship of the family of Christ. Jesus spoke of it when he said, "Whosoever shall do the will of my Father which is in heaven, the same is my brother, and sister, and mother" (Matt. 12:50). No man, in other words, can long serve Christ without discovering among like-minded men and women a new relationship like that of happy brothers and sisters in one household (Mark 10:29-30).

It is like a motherless boy whose father was an itinerant doctor among certain Indians. When the boy's elder brother and sister were sent to New York to school, the boy asked his father whether he might go with him on his journeys. So they took two horses and traveled together. Day after day the bones in the boy's body ached from riding. Often he was thirsty. Often he was hot, and often cold. The boy thought of his brother and sister. He told himself that they had never endured what he was enduring. Then he began to feel sorry, not for himself, but for them.

For as the boy and his father rode, they talked of many things. And the boy was filled with admiration for this man whom he had scarcely known, who was so wise and gentle, who brought healing to so many people. One day, therefore, when the father asked the boy whether he was lonely without his brother and sister, the boy replied, "I think that I am happier, going like this with you, than I was when they were here and you were away. And I would not change places with them now for anything."

About this time the father began to give the boy simple tasks that he could attend to when they called at the homes of the sick. The boy, for example, would hold a light where his father needed it. Or he would find his father's instruments and hand them to him. Or he would run an errand for a patient who was in bed.

So the Indians grew fond of the boy, as earlier they had become fond of the father. They called the boy "the little doctor." They welcomed him with gladness in their homes. Thus "the little doctor" formed friendships which were closer than he had had with his own brother and sister.

But the physician in the story is Christ. And the boy is any lonely man who says to Christ, "Let me go with you and help you." And those new friends are the "members of the household of God" (Eph. 2:19 R.S.V.).

We shall pray in time of perplexity as to our duty.

For the Bible assures us that those who seek the will of God will find it (James 1:5); that it shines brightly in Christ (John 8:12; 17:26); that, if we belong to Christ, it strongly works within our heart (Phil. 2:13); and that, so far from being impossible, it is the one thing necessary for us (I John 2:17). Moreover, Jesus himself, who knew about these things, spoke of a man's doing the will of God as though it were the natural thing to do (Luke 6:46) — under one condition. This clear proviso is that a man repent the folly of not having done the will of God earlier (Matt. 21:28-32).

So the good news is that the essential thing, for want of which life withers and is of no account, has come into the world through Christ with radiance and power. The good news is that this essential thing, if we but turn and receive it, may now be radiantly and powerfully ours. So, with penitence and thankfulness and joy, we open wide our life to the Spirit and the mind of Christ (Rom 8:9; Eph. 4:17-32. Note especially vss. 22-24).

Then much at once becomes plain: not all, but much. And this which has been clarified is, in so far, God's will both for our conscience and for our hands. Moreover, what reason has a man to complain—or to excuse himself— that in such-and-such respect his duty is unknown to him, if he has left undone those duties which are clearly manifest?

For example, long before the splendor of Christ invaded the conscience of mankind, the basic will of God was voiced by the prophet Micah, in words that have never lost their challenge, "He hath showed thee, O man, what is good; and what doth the Lord require of thee, but to do justly, and to love mercy, and to walk humbly with thy God?" (6:8.)

Jesus in his own flesh fulfilled that, filling it with new vividness and power. Jesus clarified that and gave it new light. But Jesus never contradicted that. Indeed, any seeming guidance which contravenes this basic understanding of God's will, or that enlargement of it which is in Christ, is no true guidance, but delusion.

Suppose, now, that a man should inquire as to his duty.

111

He must begin with this simple obligation. For if he deals unjustly, or if he is indifferent to mercy, or if he walks among his fellow men wrapped up in pride, striving to make the neighbors envy him, he has in this degree failed to advance in the direction of further unfolding of God's will. Which is to say, if a man does justly, and loves mercy, and walks humbly with his God, that deed and that love and that life may so clarify the man's mind as to enable him to penetrate confusion and in many instances to discern the will of God without specific instruction. But pride and pitilessness and sharp dealing blind a man, so that he stumbles in darkness at high noon (Isa. 59:7-10).

It is like a man suffering from physical exhaustion, to whom his physician said, "You must have so-much rest each day, and so-much outdoor exercise." But the man continued to work twelve hours out of twenty-four, and nightly he caroused with his friends until the dawn, and when he went into the open air it was only to ride in a closed car from one dissipation to another. After a time, therefore, the man again consulted his physician, saying, "I have a big deal coming up, and I cannot think straight about it. You must give me something that will clear my mind."

But the doctor answered the man, "Have you taken the rest which I prescribed? Have you daily exercised outdoors? If you had done these things, you would now be able to think clearly. What do you suppose can substitute for these basic practices?"

Similarly, when we would discover the unknown will of God, our first step is to do the will of God which is already clear. By so doing we learn that if we obey when God speaks, we need not be anxious when God is silent. For to

112

heed what God says is to be sufficiently instructed as to what he does not say.

Even for his loved ones God does not post lighted lamps along the length of life's path, so that they may look ahead at them, shining through the night, and see the ups and downs and convolutions of the way. Instead God places a lantern in our hand (Ps. 119:105), and says in effect, Follow the high trail and I will journey with you (John 14:23). But the lamp does not reveal the path a mile ahead of us. It throws light before our feet. Then our obedience in walking the first mile causes the light to shine upon that spot, a mile from our beginning, which was earlier wrapped in darkness. And God, who has accompanied our going forth, is with us still. And if at some joining of the way, our consecrate intelligence, aided by the light which God has given, should be unable to distinguish between two seeming-equal paths, then God may take our hand and lead us (Ps. 139:10) or he may speak to us directly, as it is written, "And thine ears shall hear a word behind thee, saying, This is the way, walk ye in it, when ye turn to the right hand, and when ye turn to the left" (Isa. 30:21).

Thus the will of God is known as light within our mind and before our feet, and as a gentle pressure on our hand, and as a quiet inward voice. The will of God is known also in providence (Isa. 42:16) —which is to say, in the opening and closing of opportunity. Not every open door, to be sure, is opened of God. Some open doors are invitations to evil. Always those openings and closings which are providential are in agreement with the light of Christ which is within us. And when God draws us by the hand or whispers in our heart, those invitations and denials which he inspires round about us concur, likewise, with that.

It is like a small boy who, as he set out for school, was asked by his father to do an errand at the bank on the way home. But when the boy arrived at the bank, the door was closed and locked. Then the boy remembered that school and bank ended their day at the same hour. So the boy was filled with confusion as to his duty, and with questioning as to his father's wisdom. However, while the boy stood wondering, the door before him opened and a kindly voice said, "Come on in! Your father telephoned, so we have been expecting you."

Yet how much greater than the authority of that boy's earthly parent is the authority of our Father who is in heaven! Paul says of him that he is "above all and through all and in all" (Eph. 4:6 R.S.V.). And the author of the Revelation writes of him in Christ as One who "openeth, and no man shutteth; and shutteth, and no man openeth" (3:7).

So we take heart, assured that where God wills a child of his to go, there he wills also the necessary opening of doors; and that when need arises, he closes other doors against us, saving us for his own purpose. Discernment of the will of God, therefore, is the work of Christian wisdom. But Christian wisdom becomes ours in part through Christian prayer (Col. 1:9-14).

This is not to suggest that the will of God is always easy to do. There may be thorns and a cross for him who prays, "Thy will be done" (Matt. 6:10; 26:39). Yet, in its issue, defiance of the will of God is harder than obedience. For the thorns that are of disobedience are deep within the

114

conscience. And the cross that is of selfishness must be borne by a man alone.

We shall pray in success and happiness.

For we shall overflow with thankfulness, knowing that in so far as success and happiness be genuine, they come from him who is the author of every good and perfect gift (James 1:17).

Here is perhaps the given time in which to cultivate a certain kind of prayer. This is an extension of our other prayers, which may become a blessing, not only in happiness, but also in loneliness and grief. It is connected with a certain way of seeing, in which we note the little things, the tiny goodnesses of every day; and, at the moment of perception, ejaculate a prayer of thankfulness.

Commonly so much of beauty fails to stir our wonder: a curving branch, the song of a sparrow, light on a puddle. So much of kindness leaves us hard and cold: the patience of a bus driver, the smile of a child. So much of comfort goes unnoticed: the warmth or welcome coolness of a room, the shining of a candle. So we ask God to open our eyes with the undimmed vision of little ones, that we may see the innumerable company of blessings by which we are encompassed. Thus our happiness will be multiplied and we shall praise God anew.

But in success and happiness we remember those who are without success and from whom happiness is far removed. Then we make an offering to God of the success and happiness which he has given us. "For unto whomsoever much is given, of him shall be much required: and to whom men have committed much, of him they will ask the more." (Luke 12:48.)

So we pray that our mind may be illumined, our heart disturbed, our will aroused, until this success and happiness of ours be used as a trust from God for the benefit of the discouraged and unhappy. Thus success will become more than success: it will be made an instrument of healing. And our happiness will be deepened into the blessedness of the children of God.

It is like a young man who won a prize, who then remembered a blind friend. So the young man gave his money to a skilled surgeon, and those sightless eyes were restored to sight.

But if success fills us with vainglory (Jer. 9:23-24), so that instead of offering it in thankfulness to God for his merciful use, we flaunt it in the faces of our fellow men, it then becomes a peril to ourself and an offense to heaven and earth.

It is like another man who won a prize. This man straightway visited the homes of all his friends and acquaintances, many of whom had families, many of whom had striven for the award which this young man had won. He waved the prize money in his hand. "Look, folks!" he cried, "I'm smart! I have a thousand dollars here! Boy, am I happy!" And he spent the money in drunkenness and harlotry.

So in success and happiness, if we be wise, we fall upon our knees.

Yet not throughout our gladness only, but in every circumstance, at the core of all petition, we plead for enlightenment and strengthening, that our prayers may be-

116

come such as God desires to hear—and grant. Then our longing is fulfilled, as he whom we seek comes graciously to us, and stoops, and enters the opened temple of our heart (Mal. 3:1), and teaches us to pray (Gal. 4:6; Rom. 8:15, 16, 26).

SOME AIDS TO PRAYER

Books of Original Prayers

Altar Stairs,[1] by Joseph Fort Newton. New York: The Macmillan Company, 1937. These prayers of gentle loveliness should help many. They are dedicated to those who, "weary of seeking without finding, are willing to walk the quiet way of prayer."

A Diary of Private Prayer, by John Baillie. New York: Charles Scribner's Sons, 1936. Here are morning and evening prayers for thirty-one days and a Sunday. This book is a classic of personal devotion. To be sure, even a classic, unless it happens to appeal to us, is of small value in our own life. But this book has appealed to more than a few.

Lift Up Your Hearts, by Walter Russell Bowie. New York and Nashville: Abingdon Press, 1956. Here are meditations, prayers, and litanies both for adults and for young people. The topics cover a wide variety of needs and important seasons of the year. There is a simplicity about these prayers which is at first deceptive, like the clarity of a mountain lake. But one who dives in finds that there is depth.

Prayers of the Christian Life, by John Underwood Stephens. New York: Oxford University Press, 1952. Here are prayers for many occasions, including morning, noon, evening; mealtime; wakefulness; sorrow; suffering and sickness; seasons of the Christian year. There are petitions, intercessions, confessions, and thanksgivings. This is a companion volume to *A Simple Guide to Prayer.*

Prayers of the Spirit,[2] by John Wallace Suter. New York: Harper & Brothers, 1943. These prayers are short, mostly in "collect" form. They are marked by broad understanding and unusual purity of expression. Some of these prayers are among the most beautiful of their kind in the English language.

The Temple, by W. E. Orchard. New York: E. P. Dutton & Company, Inc., 1946. In these prayers are mingled aspiration, joyful communion, adoration. They run deep. They reach high.

[1] Reported out of print at the time of this writing. But such books may be reprinted or, if not, may sometimes be bought secondhand or may be found in a library.

[2] *Ibid.*

Anthologies of Prayer

The Book of Prayers, edited by Leon and Elfrieda McCauley. New York: Crown Publishers, Inc., 1954. This book is available in two editions. One is paper-covered and sells in dime stores. This edition is put out by the Dell Publishing Company, Inc. Here are prayers under three main heads: for adults, for young people, for little children. The very modest price of this book should make it possible for it to be in every home.

A Chain of Prayer Across the Ages, by Selina Fitzherbert Fox. New York: E. P. Dutton & Company, Inc., 1941. These selections have been garnered from forty centuries of prayer. This book should bring enrichment to anyone who uses it.

Prayers for Living, compiled by Hazel T. Wilson. New York and Nashville: Abingdon Press, 1955. This is a thin book of vest-pocket size. It may be had in a binding of attractive blue leather-ette for $1.00, as of this date; or in genuine red leather with gilt-edged pages for not too much more. These prayers, many of which are well known, but some of which are brand new, are arranged as morning and evening devotions for thirty days. A very handy book.

The Student Prayerbook, edited and written by a Haddam House committee under chairmanship of John Oliver Nelson. New York: Association Press, 1953. These prayers are grouped as devotions for fourteen days, morning and evening; as prayers in connection with Bible study; as prayers in connection with life on the campus, vocation and careers, the Church, the world; and as general prayers.

Service Books

These books of the various denominations often contain prayers for family use. Moreover, many of the prayers printed in the services of public worship, or grouped under special heads, are suitable for personal devotion.

Books About Prayer

The Life of Prayer,[3] by Baron Friedrich von Hügel. New York: E. P. Dutton & Company, Inc., 1929. This book consists of two

[3] *Ibid.*

lectures by Baron von Hügel which were published in the second series of his *Essays and Addresses on the Philosophy of Religion*. They are closely reasoned, devout, luminous. One feels upon reading them that one is in the presence of a soul made radiant by that communion which is the subject of the lectures.

The Lord's Prayer, by E. F. Scott. New York: Charles Scribner's Sons, 1951. Here, by an outstanding New Testament scholar, is a clear, perceptive, and scholarly discussion of the prayer that Jesus taught, containing, inevitably, much that is of value for all prayer.

The Lower Levels of Prayer, by George Stewart. New York and Nashville: Abingdon Press, 1940. Here is advice that is simple and practical for the beginner. Yet if the wisdom in this book were taken to heart and incorporated into life, one would not long remain upon prayer's "lower levels."

Prayer, by George Arthur Buttrick. New York and Nashville: Abingdon Press, 1942. No one who is willing to exercise his mind on the matter, while broadening and deepening his experience of prayer, should miss this book.

Prayer,[4] by Friedrich Heiler, translated and edited by Samuel McComb and J. Edgar Park. New York: Oxford University Press, 1932. The subtitle of this book is "A Study in the History and Psychology of Religion." It may be "on the heavy side" for a mind untrained in academic discipline. But for those who are up to it, it offers a rich vein of pure treasure, to be mined with thankfulness and wonder. Here prayer is traced from primitive society through early civilization into its place in modern philosophical thought, in the experience of great personalities, in the mystics and in the prophets, in public worship and in personal life.

Prayer and the Common Life, by Georgia Harkness. New York and Nashville: Abingdon Press, 1948. This is a wonderfully clear and simple exposition of the ways of prayer as seen in relation to the major affirmations of present-day theology and psychology.

Your Prayers Are Always Answered, by Alexander Lake. New York: Gilbert Press, Inc., 1956. This book, the result of wide-ranging inquiry, is a record of answered prayers. The stories are simply, clearly, and often movingly, told. To be sure, readers may differ as to the interpretation to be placed upon this or that incident, but the central thesis is well sustained: that when our lives are offered

[4] *Ibid.*

121

to God, he, even through seeming coincidence, takes charge of them.

The Bible

King James Version. London, 1611. Probably no other rendering of Scripture, except the Latin Vulgate, possesses such rhythmical grandeur of language. Yet the primary mission of the Bible to the soul is not to make a beautiful sound but to make breathtaking sense, and unfortunately the sense of the King James Version is ever and again obscured beneath words which today are used with different meanings from those intended by the King James' translators. But whereas many of us know that we do not know Latin, because the words are obviously strange to us, we do not know that we do not know seventeenth-century English, because the words appear to be familiar. So we force today's meanings into ancient words, and thus unknowingly distort their sense, meanwhile assuring ourself that we understand it.

Again, modern scholarship has at its disposal manuscripts much nearer to the original than those available to the King James' committee. Accordingly, if we use this seventeenth-century version, as indeed has been done in this book, we shall correct it where it falls short, by means of something else that is more accurate.

The Revised Standard Version. New York: Thomas Nelson & Sons, 1952. Taken all in all, this is perhaps the most satisfactory rendition of the Scriptures to be had in English. For one who does not wish to use it alone it makes an invaluable corrective to the King James. It may be had in the New Testament, or in separate volumes for the Old Testament and the New, or in one volume containing the whole Bible.

The New Testament, an American Translation, by Edgar J. Goodspeed. Chicago: University of Chicago Press, 1923. This is one of the happiest of those translations of Scripture which have been made by one man working alone. Done in definitely "American" English, Dr. Goodspeed's work has opened the New Testament to large numbers of people. Although it is written without the stiffness which is sometimes associated with the Bible, this translation is thrillingly faithful to the Greek original, even where it employs a whole clause to give the meaning of one word. Yet it is not "wordy." It fairly races along.

The Bible, an American Translation, containing the Old Testament translated by a group of scholars under the editorship of J. M. Powis Smith and the New Testament by Edgar J. Goodspeed (as above). Chicago: University of Chicago Press, 1931.

The Holy Bible, a New Translation, by James Moffatt. New York: Harper & Brothers, 1926. This is the work of one man throughout. It is done in "English" English, as against the "American" English of Smith-Goodspeed. It may be had in the New Testament alone or in a single volume containing the whole Bible.

Books About the Bible

The Abingdon Bible Commentary. New York and Nashville: Abingdon Press, 1929. This book contains not only a concise exposition of the Bible but also fine introductory chapters on each of the Bible's books, in addition to generous background material for both the Old Testament and the New, as well as articles on the Bible as a whole.

The Bible Speaks to You, by Robert McAfee Brown. Philadelphia: The Westminster Press, 1955. This is the kind of explanation of the essential nature of the Bible that many have wanted. It is simple, reverent, scholarly, and very lively. The main theme: how God meets us in the Bible, and what this meeting means in terms of modern life. If one could have but one book about the message of the Bible, this might well be it.

The Bible Today. New York: Harper & Brothers, 1956. Its languages, archaeology, manuscripts, translations, and editions; its contributions to religion, music, literature, and the common life—discussed by twenty-eight authorities. The publishers have stated the case for this book, in part, as follows: "Twenty-nine brief, fact-packed articles, each by a leading authority, summarize the latest findings in every major field of Biblical study, leaving aside all theological dispute." There are many illustrations.

How to Read the Bible, by Frederick C. Grant. New York: Morehouse-Gorham Company, 1956. The noted New Testament scholar and professor of biblical theology at Union Theological Seminary, New York, disposes of certain misunderstandings about the Bible and points out helpful ways of studying it.

The Story of the New Testament, by Edgar J. Goodspeed. Chicago: University of Chicago Press, 1916. Here the separate books of the New Testament are considered in the probable order of their composition, as Dr. Goodspeed sees it, with illuminating comment upon the circumstances of their origin and with analysis of their contents. The corresponding volume is *The Story of the Old Testament.* Or the two may be had in one binding, under the title *The Story of the Bible.*